Just-A-Cottage

Also by Kendall McDonald

THE WHITE BATON

RED SKY AT NIGHT

SPEARFISHING IN BRITAIN

THE WRECK HUNTERS

THE UNDERWATER BOOK (edited)

HOW TO GET MORE FUN FROM YOUR BOAT

THE SECOND UNDERWATER BOOK (edited)

MORE THAN SKIN DEEP

FISHWATCHING AND PHOTOGRAPHY

THE WRECK DETECTIVES

VIVA PENELOPE !

THE WORLD UNDERWATER BOOK (edited)

THE INFLATABLE BOAT BOOK

THE TREASURE DIVERS

FOOD FROM THE SEASHORE

Kendall McDonald

More Than
Just-A-Cottage

Sevenoaks
ASHGROVE PRESS

Revised and augmented edition
First published in Great Britain by Ashgrove Press Ltd.
25 Quakers Hall Lane, Sevenoaks, Kent TN13 3TU
1981

ISBN 0 906798 13 2

Set in eleven on twelve point Baskerville
Printed and bound in Great Britain by
Biddles Ltd., Guildford and Kings Lynn
on paper supplied by Frank Grunfeld Ltd, London

Contents

List of Illustrations

Diagrams

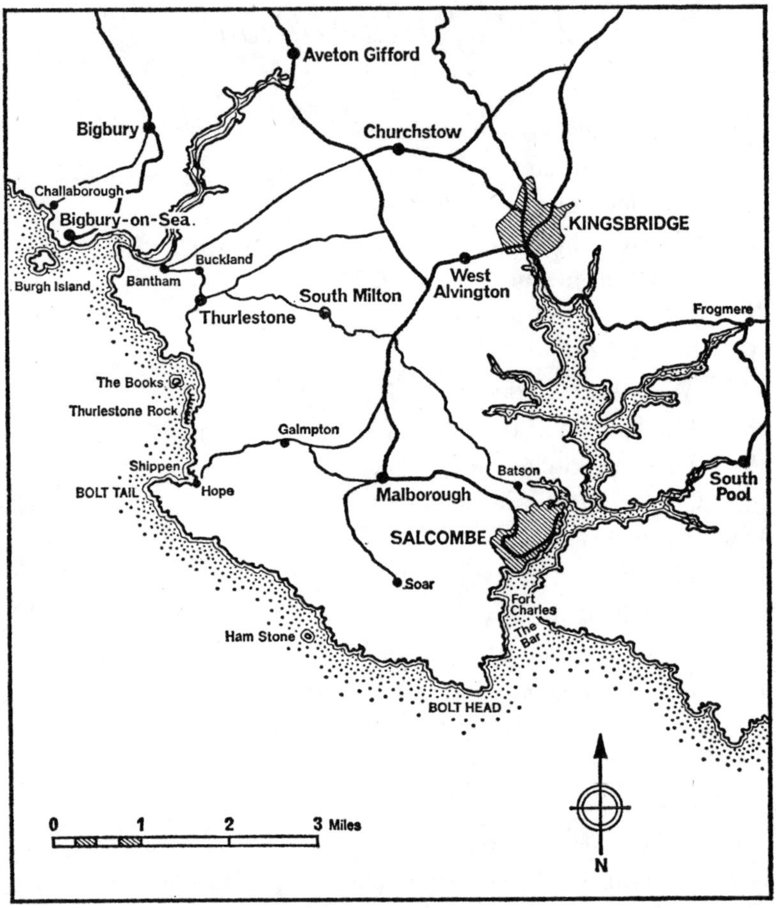

Aveton Gifford
Bigbury
Churchstow
Challaborough
Bigbury-on-Sea
KINGSBRIDGE
Burgh Island
Bantham
Buckland
Thurlestone
South Milton
West Alvington
Frogmere
The Books
Thurlestone Rock
Galmpton
Shippen
BOLT TAIL
Hope
Malborough
Batson
South Pool
SALCOMBE
Soar
Fort Charles
The Bar
Ham Stone
BOLT HEAD
0
1
2
3 Miles
N

Introduction

The Cottage Out of Control

This is the story of a cottage that got out of control. The story, not the cottage!

I did try to confine this book to my cottage in Thurlestone, South Devon, but it can't be done. You see, no old building is as simple as that. Once you start to try to find out about it, you are launched, not only into the lives of the people who lived in it before you, but into the lives of those who passed by the door.

For the people who passed by were making the history of the area, just as much as those who stayed in the cottage and lived out their lives under the old and blackened beams.

So, once the door of the cottage was opened to it, my story went rushing out into the South Devon countryside. To keep up with it, I have had to find out all sorts of extraordinary things.

I have had to locate the Iron Age fort which looked down on Hope Cove. I have had to study the Domesday Book of William the Conqueror – because Thurlestone existed then.

Once you have seen it, nothing could be more distinctive as a landmark than the archway of Thurlestone Rock. So it is not surprising to find that the Rock is in the Domesday Book – as Torlestan. I drew the line at learning Saxon, but I am reliably informed that this name is taken from the Saxon word 'thyrl' meaning 'a hole'. So we have 'Hole-stone' and then finally, of course, Thurlestone.

But if my story didn't force me to learn Saxon, it did drive me into the world of old documents.

I have pored over the records, written with a quill pen in the state cabin of some long-gone man-o'war, when a poor unfortunate was being court-martialled for the loss of his ship and nearly 600 men on the savage rocks of Bolt Tail.

I know now that some of those who passed by my cottage door had blood on their hands – the blood of a woman whom they had killed in the surf of Thurlestone Sands.

Know, too, that Kipling's 'Watch the wall, my darling, while the Gentlemen go by!' was no idle instruction as far as Thurlestone, Bantham and Salcombe were concerned. The 'Gentlemen' were very active in these parts and even kept fifty barrels of brandy at a time in Thurlestone Church. Brandy for the Parson, 'baccy for the Clerk, indeed!

So, apart from studying the history of smuggling in the West Country, my cottage story has led me to all sorts of footpaths, footpads, fantasies and facts. My cottage has stood for the King, fallen for Parliament, and still been there to see the Monarchy restored.

My cottage, I suspect, was there when the Armada sailed down the Channel harassed by Drake and Frobisher and Hawkins. It was there too when one of those Armada ships, which had circumnavigated the British Isles, was driven ashore in Hope Cove with no one strong enough to steer away from the savage revenge of the local inhabitants.

If they brought beams from the ship to Thurlestone, did they also drive the prisoners up the village street on their way to gaol in Kingsbridge? I don't know. But I do know that men from Thurlestone, Bantham, and Salcombe were in practically every major British naval engagement from then on.

I think that if you read this book, you will realise that far from being just a clutch of sleepy, beautiful villages – because this is the most beautiful part of Britain – the South Hams are living history.

I told you that my story had got out of control. I do not regret it. Finding out about my cottage has opened up to me the world of antiques, of stripping furniture, of brass fittings, of Jack the Ripper, of my family, and of practically everything you can think of that has to do with life.

But, most important of all, it has opened up to me a world where people want to help, want to tell you about the past, want to be craftsmen, want, in fact, to be wanted. And you can't have anything more enjoyable than that!

KENDALL McDONALD,
Just-a-Cottage,
Thurlestone,
South Devon.

1. Uncle Charlie – Postman Extraordinary

I didn't want a cottage. Not a thatched one. Not a tiled one. Not an old one. Not even a new one.

Possessions, I felt until quite recently, were just a nuisance if you exceeded the basic minimum. And a second home was certainly such an excess. Running one house was bad enough. Two would be twice the trouble – and the further away the second home, cottage or villa was, so the trouble would be bound to increase out of all proportion.

It was this sort of feeling that had made me turn down – gaily, because we were standing in a bar at the time – the offer of two villas on the hillside overlooking Aiguablava, without doubt the most beautiful bay on the Costa Brava of Spain. At £3,000 each all those years ago, the villas were undoubtedly a snip. In fact I saw them last year and they are certainly worth £20,000 apiece today.

At the time I had no regrets, even when the proposition was repeated in the cold hungover light of mid-morning.

To be honest, to have raised £6,000 then would have been just as difficult as finding £40,000 now, but it wasn't really on those grounds that I turned the offer down for the second time. It was all too much trouble.

I even made up a new version of useful phrases to replace the old Baedecker guide book classic of 'My postilion has been struck by lightning, please direct me to the nearest doctor'. One of the best was, I thought, 'My villa has been blown away by a typhoon, please help me to remove it from the second floor of the Splendide Hotel'.

Seriously, I did think that distance must lend disenchantment to the holiday home-owner. Operating at long range to replace a roof – even if the second home was in a remote part of this country – would obviously be an affair of raised blood-pressure on the owner's part and sublime indifference on the part of the locals.

So you can see that I was hardly ideal country cottage material.

Now, my sister Christine is exactly the opposite. For years – until she got her own Holly Cottage in Sturminster Marshall, Dorset – cottages were the world of her day-dreams. Books about cottages, plans of cottages, cottage furniture drawings, and pictures of other people's cottages were her reading food. And I sometimes felt that her car was only a pumpkin which had turned into a coach to take her to view one tumbledown cottage after another. All of which my other sister, Mavis, viewed with the kind of cool detachment that only a love of real modern central heating can bring about.

So Mavis and I would joke about Christine's cottage obsession and the idea of actually owning a cottage was, as far as I was concerned, as remote as . . . well, it is difficult these days to think of anything far enough away.

How is it, then, that I am the proud owner of a little thatched cottage in South Devon?

Obviously I am a man who had to eat not only his words, but also his earlier ideas. It happened like this. . . .

My grandfather, William Kendall Hill, pounded a beat in Jack the Ripper's London. It was a world not far removed from the swirling fogs and sordid slums of Hollywood's film versions. As a child I can remember my mother chiding him for telling us stories about those days.

His favourite story – and that of my mother when she thought I and my sisters were not around – was of the night when he almost discovered one of the Ripper's victims. He said that during the time of the Ripper's reign of terror, policemen were ordered to patrol in twos. He was detailed off to a beat near the area where other victims had been found.

As they walked – and you can imagine their boots thumping along in the dark – they came to a junction in the roads. His companion suggested that they should split and rejoin where the road came together again. My grandfather protested that this was against orders, but his fellow 'Bobby' sneered at him, suggesting he was scared.

So they parted and my grandfather waited anxiously when

the meeting place was reached. Finally his waiting ended as a police whistle shrilled through the night – his companion had found another of the Ripper's victims and had only just missed meeting the Ripper face to face!

Looking back on it now, I know that the story was a certain heart-stopper – especially when listened to at the edges of the oil-lamp's light – but it would get embroidered in each telling until Jack the Ripper slit the other policeman's throat and my grandfather was fortunate to have escaped with his life. I suppose the story depended to a large degree on the amount of rough cider that my grandfather had taken before the telling.

By the time I heard the story my grandfather had retired and had taken his family down to live in Thurlestone in South Devon. He bought a house called 'Woodbine' and eked out his pension there by taking in paying guests.

It is always difficult to find out exactly what happened in the past – even if you have the family letters to study, because people only write about the things that concern them at the time, and not the background to the events which they describe. So, anything I tell you about those days of Victorian England is the best that I can do on the evidence available. And much of the evidence available is that of my memory and of others concerned.

I know, for example, that the Hills, my grandparents had a large number of children. And little black-edged mourning cards and small overgrown graves bear testimony to the fact that today's generation know not when they are well off.

Survivors of course there were. My mother, for one. My Uncle Charlie and my Auntie Edie, to name two more. But there were others who rated no more than a sad entry in the front of the family Bible.

When the family moved from London to Devon, I know, because my mother told me, and because my grandfather's simple budget notes bear her out, that there were great adjustments to be made. With a guaranteed pension my grandfather's lot was not a particularly hard one. But he had to take in lodgers – and despite his police record he seems to have been a particularly trusting soul. Letter after letter to one particular guest who had failed to pay his bill reveals a surprising lack of wordly knowledge for a policeman.

Perhaps it was this unlikely soft side of his character which enabled him to be absorbed easily into the life of Thurlestone. It is clear that a Devon village in those days must have had a remarkable ability to absorb people – though, mind you, the choice of Thurlestone for my grandfather's retirement was not one of sheer luck. The Hills had come from South Devon originally. There were relatives in places round about, though Victorian standard-pose yellowing photographs, which I found in a trunk, are the only evidence of their passing. And that is the trouble with old photographs. The people who treasured them at the time knew who people were and rarely bothered to write on the back their Christian names let alone surnames.

So South Devon absorbed the Hills. So much so that though my mother stayed in London and worked as a seamstress, young Charlie Hill, my uncle, was taken from a London school and sent straight into direct confrontation with the pupils of a school in Kingsbridge. He found their accents comic; they must have found his appalling. But Charlie was a mimic. He aped them, teased them – and then suddenly found that the soft burrs of Devon had stuck to him so firmly that he never spoke any other way for the rest of his life.

By the time the 1914-18 war came, Charlie Hill was such a Devonian that there could be only one regiment for him – The Devonshires.

Private, later Corporal, C. Hill, No. 240754 of 'A' Company of the 1/5th Devons saw quite a lot of that war. He fought 'Johnny Turk' in Palestine, was there when Gaza fell and pushed on to Jerusalem. Was switched suddenly to the British Expeditionary Force in France and, because of such a sudden change of climate, fell an easy victim to the influenza which killed as easily as bomb or bullet.

Once recovered from this, it was back to the trenches and his 'Blighty one' – he took a small piece of shrapnel in his right shoulder and was evacuated just before the end of the war to England. Once discharged, he tried to join the Great Western Railway, but nothing seems to have come of it and so he became a postman. He had one extra qualification that is not required of any postman. He could always tell when it was going to rain – the shrapnel left in his shoulder would start to ache hours before!

So Charlie Hill, ex-corporal of the Devonshires, was now Thurlestone's postman – and the postman for many surrounding villages – working outwards from the main office in Kingsbridge.

I have told you something about my family, my uncle and how they came to be connected with the beautiful village of Thurlestone, simply because the cottage that I now own used to belong to my uncle Charlie – village postman extraordinary. If you do not know the background you will never quite understand the forces that drove me from my active avoidance of a second home into cottage ownership.

My grandfather, William Kendall Hill, had bought 'Woodbine', which is set back from the main hill of Thurlestone Village and is approached from the main road by a passageway underneath one of the bedrooms of 'Just-a-Cottage', a tiny thatched cottage almost opposite the road which leads to Bantham.

I said earlier that my grandfather was not entirely a stranger to Devon. His brother, Henry Hill, who was also a retired Police Inspector (it seems to have run in the family), owned property in Plymouth and left some of this to his brother.

Together with 'Woodbine', my grandfather had bought 'Just-a-Cottage' and so, when Charlie announced he was getting married, he was able to transfer the cottage over to him for the couple to set up home. The transfer was made on November 2nd, 1931. Charlie Hill, postman, married Violet Beatrice Bevell, spinster, on February 16th and 'Just-a-Cottage' became their home.

No, that isn't quite true. The cottage at that time had no name. 'Just-a-Cottage' was named then by either my aunt or my uncle. I can't tell you now whose idea it was to call it 'Just-a-Cottage' .But the name suits it perfectly. It is tiny. It is just a cottage.

My Uncle Charlie wore his postman's hat back to front, always had a pipe stuck in his mouth, and rode his round mounted on the oldest motor-bike it is possible to imagine. The lamp on the front needed constant feeding with carbide to keep up the gas supply to the flickering flame. I should add that he only wore his hat that way when riding his motor-bike or when, off duty, playing clock golf on the sloping lawn in front of the great purple-pink fuchsia hedge in the garden of 'Woodbine'.

I can see him now. He really did have twinkling eyes and needed little encouragement to join us in a game of golf once he had parked the big stuttering bike by the little cottage in the grounds of 'Woodbine'. In that same cottage the great cider casks of my grandfather stretched tubbily from floor to rafters.

The cider never attracted Uncle Charlie – he was, I think, teetotal, even through his army life. But a game of golf on the lawn was a different matter and he would chuckle happily as some impossible shot from the bumpy ground uphill on the side way from the sea would roll incredibly into the pot for a hole in one.

We spent all our holidays at Thurlestone. All our summer ones, that is, and in childhood memory I can never remember it raining. It must have done, but it is true that when the storm clouds gather back over Dartmoor and swoop down on Salcombe on one side and Bigbury on the other, then the sun shines on in Thurlestone. It has the best weather of any part of Devon.

Our holidays were times of great excitement – particularly the start. Great trunks would be piled up in the dining room of our house in Dulwich and my sisters and I would be dressed for the journey hours before the time of departure, which was always set so that we could catch the midnight train out of Paddington.

Once at Kingsbridge the real holiday began. Up on the roof of the single-decker green Western National bus would go all our trunks and cases, and then we were off down narrow high-banked lanes winding through red-earth country.

Oh, the excitement of it all! It was especially thrilling when the bus came face to face with a farm cart or small car. The car would usually back, but for the carts the bus driver would sometimes wiggle his bus backwards into a parking place as though it was one of today's Minis.

Finally, the bus would stop on the steep hill right outside the passageway entrance to 'Woodbine', blocking off the door of 'Just-a-Cottage'. And the big figure of my grandfather in dark waistcoat would be there to meet us. With him, just behind the big iron gate into the passageway, would be the tiny figure of my grandmother, Elizabeth.

I was a bit afraid of my grandfather, much more of my grandmother who could be a proper wasp if she tried. But I was not so afraid of either of them that I let it spoil the holiday.

First, we would go through the performance of unloading all the trunks. The bus-driver would call my grandfather, 'Mr 'ill', and in turn my grandfather would know everyone on the bus. It was a scene of great confusion, but no one ever struck me as being in a hurry, and finally the trunks would be manhandled through the passage, under the signs my Uncle Charlie had painted donkeys' years ago: 'Welcome the Coming' said the sign facing us as we went in, and if you turned your head to look back, the sign you would see at that end of the tunnel was 'Speed the Parting Guest'.

Then we would be out of the cool of the passageway, into the sun of the back-yard of 'Woodbine'. The holiday had begun.

What holidays they were – in memory at least. And to remember them so fondly must mean that we did enjoy them.

There seemed so much to do. I was always sent up to bed with my own flickering candle. Behind me I left the warmth of the kitchen with its great glowing stove. I didn't really like the climb up the back-stairs to my bed. The candle flickered creating frightening shadows on the white-washed walls, and when my mother came up to tuck me in and the candle was put out and I was left alone, the darkness was the darkest thing you can imagine.

It is the same today. When lights are out in Thurlestone, real darkness falls. At first your eyes fail to cope with the loss of street-lighting, but slowly the light of country night is enough to navigate the lanes and fields. The village street becomes a grey ribbon leading from the Post Office down to the Thurlestone Hotel.

And, though it will spoil a great deal of our enjoyment, visitors should know that the village street itself acts as a trumpet, magnifying whispers and turning low conversation into shouts for those who lie abed in the cottages. In fact, the lurid details of visitors' sex lives that emerge as they trudge from village inn up to guest house is a constant source of amusement. But Devon air is a drug and despite this impromptu cabaret, sleep comes easily to those used to city-grimed, thin, low-oxygen level atmosphere.

We slept heavily as children, even though London then had nothing like the same traffic fumes and noisy nights. My Thurlestone memories are concerned in the main with the sea, with butterflies and later with the war.

The sea, because our daily journey – and thinking back, it must have been exhausting for my mother – was either to Leas Foot or Yarmer Sands (to find those on today's maps you must look not for Yarmer, but for Yarmouth).

Leas Foot was my favourite. For it was there that we had found the Tunnel. I remember this as a giant cave of dark pools and dripping walls. It would only appear when the tide was out. And to make it even more exciting, the floor of part of the cave was the top of the concrete casing over the pipe which carried a stream out to sea. This stream was the same one which meandered down to the sea past the front of the Golf Club and which had wire-netting over it in many places to stop too great a loss of golf balls.

My sister Christine would creep happily through the Tunnel, next would come a not-so-confident me, and following timidly behind would be my younger sister, Mavis. Once through the Tunnel, you were face to face with the sea and I can remember what an impressive sight it was. There were two ways back. One was through the dark gloom of the cave again; the other was to climb a vast mountainous peak through which the Tunnel had been cut by sharp Devon seas.

It was a world of sun, sea, sand, rock pools and, of course, The Tunnel. And always waiting for our safe return, ready to wrap us in huge towels, whose soft pile smelt of home and somehow of the sea, was my mother.

I know that in childish memory things always seem bigger than they are. I am used to childhood forests turning into three trees and some low bushes, but I was not prepared, on a recent return trip, to find that The Tunnel, scene of childhood bravery turned out to be something that I would not mind creeping through; indeed, the sea has much enlarged it since those childhood days. But then whatever was my sister, Christine, the oldest of us all, doing in allowing us to attempt it? Looking at it now, I realise that my mother, sitting high on the shore away to the left, had no idea what we were up to.

If you wish to find our childhood adventure playground today, you should look to the right of the beach. I think you will agree that it is no sea cave, no tunnel, nothing more than a very minor hole in a very ordinary sea-cut slate rock. But, before you dismiss the whole thing as nothing more than the imagination of a child, you should know that, at the time I am talking about, there were eels to be dug out of the shingle where the pipe emerged to the sea. In fact, I took one home to Dulwich and kept it for months until it, too, decided that the sea was calling and it set off across our garden in the night never to be seen again.

I said that I thought my mother found our desire to go down to the sea exhausting. I am sure she did. Today, you have only to wheel a push-chair or pram from the Golf Club, up past the Church and the Hotel, and on to the upper limits of the village to realise that the trip once, and sometimes twice, a day is pretty killing. In these days of cars, of course, it is easier, but though the slope from village to sea is fine going down, it is still a stiff return.

We walked then. We had no car. Few people did. In that vast grey arc of early childhood memory . . . somewhere there is a protest about my sister Mavis riding when I had to walk. But I can't pull such a thought into clear recall. We had one push-chair. I think this warped my whole life. I have never liked walking and I suspect that it comes from having to climb Thurlestone hill in those days of early memory!

Mind you, if we went to Yarmer Sands, it was an easier trip. You didn't have to go so far down the hill, peeling off after passing Broad's Dairy and the Church on to a public footpath. And it was easier to get the sand from between your toes on the springy grass of the Links golf course on the way back. But I still liked Leas Foot best. What a damned nuisance I must have been!

Usually, if memory serves me right, we went down to Leas Foot. I do not think it had a great deal to do with my whimpers, whining or plaintive appeals. Looking back from adulthood to grizzling, damned-nuisance child, I now realise that we went to Lea Foot a great deal of the time because my father was playing tennis at the Club.

He was rather good. And the visiting talent was not. There can be no argument about that. A vast collection of cups and silver spoons bears testimony today to his expertise. Thurlestone, it would seem, specialised more in spoons than cups for visitors.

You see, my father was H. R. McDonald. I call him 'H.R.' rather than Henry Richard because if any man was tennis, he was. He wasn't a great smash-bang player, but rather one who relied on reliability – and a certain amount of cunning. The Thurlestone visitors were unable to cope. Indeed why should they? My father was the only journalist ever to have been made an honorary member of the All-England Club, Wimbledon's controlling body. Perhaps today I should say that he was the first ever to be accorded that honour. He reported Wimbledon for the London *Evening News* for all the years there were from Suzanne Lenglen to Billie-Jean King. He was a great man of tennis. And, unlike many journalists today, he played the game himself. Not at Wimbledon standard, but well enough to make sure that he knew exactly what he was writing about.

Thurlestone was a world of sun. We would paddle in the rock pools of Leas Foot, swim at Yarmer, or sometimes go to Thurlestone Sands, where the wide sweep of yellow starts from below the foot of the Links Hotel, now being converted to flats, and goes on to the start of the footpath that leads up over the gorse to Hope.

Thurlestone Sands were ideal for safe swimming, but I think I realise now why we went there so rarely. Push-chair wheels sink easily into the fine sand and, in addition, it was that extra bit further to go for our parents.

When we didn't go down to the sea, my father would take us a short distance up the road to Bantham, past 'Rockhill' whose round windows are made of stained glass inset into the wheels of the Reverend Peregrine Ilbert's wedding carriage*,

*The Reverend Peregrine Arthur Ilbert was Rector of Thurlestone from 1839 to 1895. I found his grand-daughter, Mrs Margaret Fawcett, living in Yealmpton and she told me of her grandfather's conversion of a barn into the fine house called 'Rockhill'. The wedding carriage wheels must have brought the family good luck – the Reverend Peregrine had nine children, seven sons and two daughters!

carry on a short way as though going down the hill, to Buckland, until we came to the butterfly tree. It drooped over the road near the entrance to the big house called 'The Downs'. For years afterwards I had always thought that this big bush was lilac with its purple flowers hanging down over the road. It amazed me that this particular spot should be the stopping place for what seemed to be all the butterflies in the world.

Big Peacocks, Red Admirals and Tortoiseshells would decorate every flower. They preened themselves in the sunshine, wings opening and closing slowly as they basked on the flowers. I know now that this was not lilac, but buddleia (or 'buddleja davidii' if you want to be technical), which was imported from Western China in the late nineteenth century and so managed to spread itself by means of tiny winged seeds that it is now described as common in Southern England. Fiendishly clever, these Chinese plants!

Not knowing, or caring, about any of that as a child, my main interest was that one could convert a small-meshed shrimping net from its rock pool use to a butterfly net without any modification whatsoever. And so I would stalk butterflies, pop them from net into jam-jar containing crushed laurel leaves from the garden, and then try to mount them artistically on pieces of cork. It was cruel and useless because clumsy childish fingers never produced an ideal specimen. It is just as well that, during today's shortage of butterflies, such occupations are less-compulsive to the television-raised child.

In my childhood another non-seaside occupation was a walk past the butterfly-tree through Ball Park across the fields to Bantham. It is still one of our favourite walks. But that too has changed. It is still magnificent with its views of Bantham, where the Avon meets the sea, and behind it Burgh Island just across from Bigbury. But when we walked this way as children, it was wilder. We would stop on the way to try and catch lizards as they sunned themselves on the dry stone walls which cut the fields in two. And succeeded only once, when to my sister Christine's horror our captive played the lizard's trick of jettisoning his tail in her fingers in order to make good his escape!

Gone with most of the stone walls is the big stream which came from Buckland. Now it seems to have disappeared underground, though it runs fast enough under the bridge near West Buckland. Perhaps this is another case of childhood memory playing the adult false. I can clearly remember being warned by my grandfather not to fall in when we leaped from stepping stone to stone across a roaring torrent which hurried on its way to Bantham and the sea.

Part of the excitement of the walk was getting to Bantham and playing amid the sand dunes and the sharp spiky grass which held them together. Bantham, though, was no place to swim. I do not remember even dipping so much as a toe in the water there. Great warning notices threatened you with death by drowning if you did. My mother and grandfather told terrible stories of poor innocents who had ignored these warnings being sucked down to ghastly death in the quicksands. I could imagine this all too clearly. As a child, imagination was not one of my weak points, and so I stuck carefully to cowboys-and-indians in the dunes and kept away from the sea. The truth, as you will read later, is that there are no quicksands at Bantham, though it is dangerous to bathe at certain times.

So through all my childhood ran the pattern of Devon life. I remember my grandfather standing by the cider barrels in the little cottage in the garden of 'Woodbine', filling glasses after Sunday morning church for his cronies. I remember my father saying how strong the brown cider was. I remember, too, being offered a sip and thinking how bitter and unpleasant it was. It was real rough cider and it bears little resemblance to the variety sold from plastic barrels in pubs today.

The after-church Sunday morning cider meeting was obviously quite a social occasion in the village. Only recently, Arthur Stidston, who lives in nearby Land Cottage, was recalling to me his boyhood memories of hunting rats in Broads Farm, near the church – one of the cornered rats leapt up and bit his father in the neck – and he too remembered his father regularly joining 'old man Hill' for cider after church. My father was a firm believer and so I – indeed the whole family – would go down the village hill to church on Sundays. It would seem to me that the whole village was there.

My father's holidays were shorter than ours, of course, and so we would stay on when he went back to work at the *Evening News*.

One holiday was different. My grandfather was ill. He had been to hospital, and was now back home. But he was not the giant I remembered. He sat in his big rocking chair in the sunshine of 'Woodbine's' porch. His head was swollen and, to me, it seemed the biggest part of him. He said little and what he did say seemed unintelligible to us children. He was scarcely able to walk and how my little grandmother coped with such a helpless giant, I will never know. The place was not the same. We had to be quiet about the house and were sent out to play whenever possible. My grandmother was more waspish with us than ever before. So we were glad to play outside.

And then, later, when we were back in London, my mother cried all day. My grandfather was dead. He had had a brain tumour. My grandmother did not survive long afterwards.

I know my mother was surprised that 'Woodbine' had been left to her. Perhaps she was the favourite daughter, and they had felt that Uncle Charlie was well provided for – who knows what inter-family pressures brought about that decision? I don't, but I think it must have caused some heartaches elsewhere in the family.

Possession of 'Woodbine' was one thing; the ability to keep it another. As a child I could not imagine that our connection with 'Woodbine' and Thurlestone could ever end – I had even heard the declaration of war that was to put both my sister Christine and myself into uniform, from a radio perched on the edge of the pulpit in Thurlestone Church (and can remember even now the face of the woman who cried during the rest of the service, as the man in Army uniform next to her tried to comfort her).

Troubles piled up for my mother. Part of 'Woodbine's' cob collapsed, almost bringing down the bedroom in which I had spent all those childhood holidays. And though the War Damage commission agreed that the damage was due to gunfire at sea and paid for a good part of it, she and my father decided they could not afford the upkeep. In about 1948, she sold 'Woodbine' for well under £2,000.

Our connection with Thurlestone was then almost severed. True, we would see Uncle Charlie and Auntie Bea whenever we were down that way, but our regular visits ceased. Uncle Charlie now drove a little red Post Office van on his village rounds, instead of the old motor-bike. We knew that he had tamed a robin to sit upon his hand during those rounds – perhaps it thought that, with his red van, he was some giant relative – but the regular exchange of news about the village that we had become accustomed to each summer ceased.

Christine was in the Wrens; later, I was in the Army. Thurlestone saw little of us. Then my mother died and we paid only rare visits to the area with my father, on the way to somewhere else.

Uncle Charlie, aged, retired, but was, I think, happy. He had his wife, 'Just-a-Cottage', and his football. And when Fulham didn't let him down, all was well.

Then Auntie Bea died and he became, to a certain extent, a recluse. Not in the sense of shunning people, but he did retire into himself. His mainstay in life was his nephew, Charles Bevell, and his wife, Elsie. And he had, of course, his neighbours. Not the neighbours of some London suburb, but real neighbours, the people of a Devon village. And a cat. A cat that didn't belong to him. A tortoiseshell cat with a limp. Uncle Charlie told me that the cat had adopted him, but I know that he did nothing to discourage it. He even built a cat-flap in his back door.

Elsie and Charles Bevell would provide him with his midday meal, but he was an independent man and would still insist on returning each night to his cottage and his television set. He fell ill, and in his last days, it was Elsie and Charles Bevell who watched over him and saw that his passing was as comfortable as possible. He died in hospital in Kingsbridge and is buried in Thurlestone Churchyard next to his wife.

For such a careful man, it is surprising that he left no will. I know, because Charles Bevell told me, that in his last hours this had worried him. I like to think that he would not have wanted some stranger in the cottage, which had been his home ever since his marriage, in the village which had been his ever since his father moved there and took young Charlie from a Fulham school and put him in a country world.

To my surprise, I was named as executor of his estate with a clear duty of putting 'Just-a-Cottage' up for auction. Or, at least, getting as much for it as was possible so that all seven other beneficiaries should get their fair share.

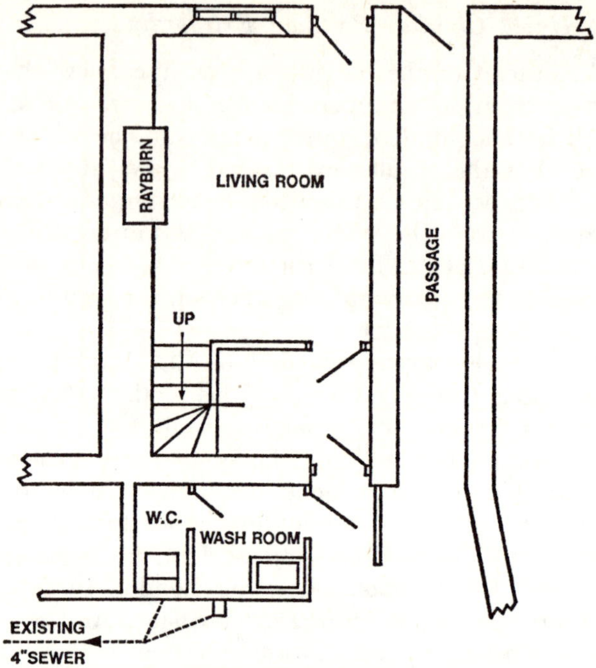

GROUND FLOOR AS IT WAS

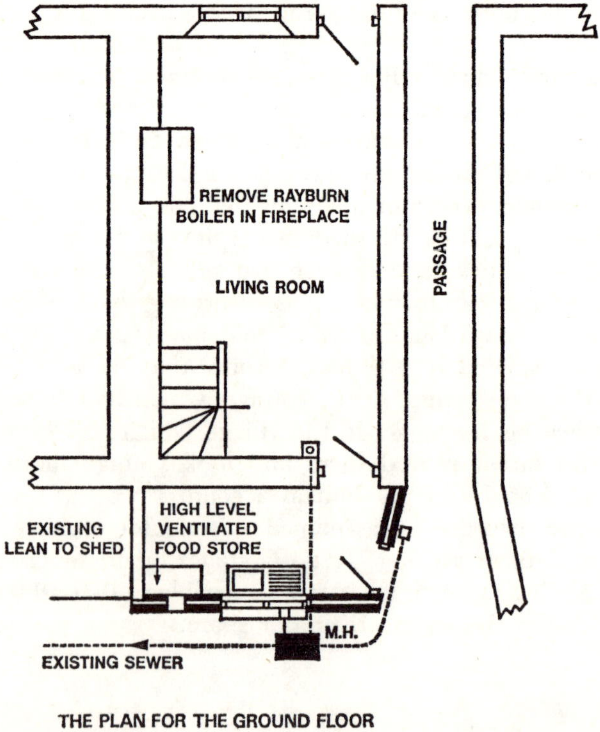

THE PLAN FOR THE GROUND FLOOR

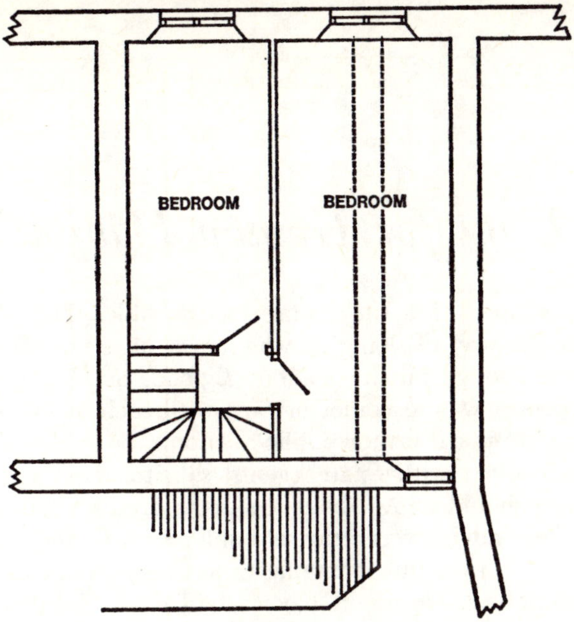

FIRST FLOOR AS IT WAS

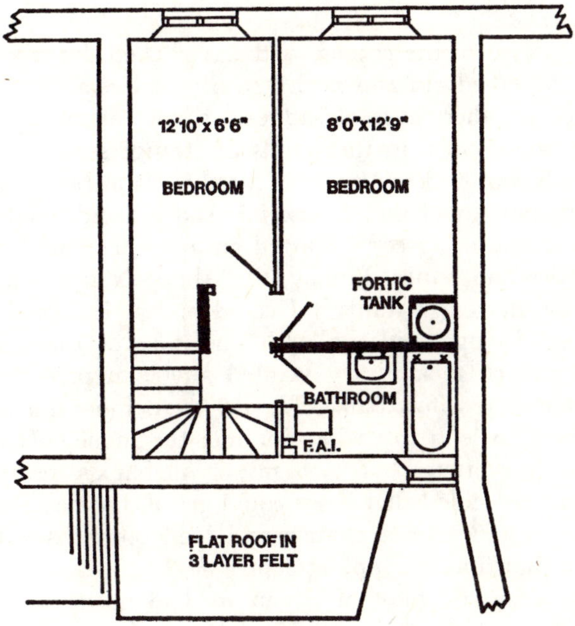

THE PLAN FOR THE FIRST FLOOR

2. *Unfit for Human Habitation*

Getting as much for the cottage as possible. That was my duty. But the way of doing so was not at all clear. The valuation on the cottage put it at about £3,000, but I felt that unless one person was to come forward with such an offer, I was duty bound to put it up for public auction.

So I consulted with estate agents, solicitors and the sort of people who should know about the ins and outs of such a procedure. Their advice was clear. A public auction might produce the valuation price, but from the things they didn't say it was equally clear that we might have a bad day. The people who should bid might not turn up – and the cottage could go for a few hundred pounds. Or if a reserve was put on, it might not reach it and a second auction was hardly likely to be more successful.

I went down to the cottage and stayed there for a week-end. Already it seemed sad and neglected. But it was at that moment that I felt another sense of sadness – a part of our family history was soon to be in the hands of strangers.

The only way to keep it in the family was to buy it. I hadn't got the money, but could I raise it? And if I did would all the other beneficiaries agree? I started on a frantic round of building societies and banks. Finally, the Abbey National agreed to provide the mortgage funds if I could find at least a third. My own bank disappointed me with airy talk of their need for liquidity (which meant they wanted any loan paid back in a year!), but my wife's bank, Lloyds, were more forthcoming. And agreed to lend my wife, not me, the money. Hurt pride was soon forgotten – but not my own bank's refusal – and Penny and I decided that if we could get all the beneficiaries to agree, we would take a chance and load ourselves with what seemed at that time a crippling debt.

All our relatives, most of whom we had not seen for years, did agree—working, presumably, on the principle that a bird in the hand was worth two unknown ones at a public auction.

And so, after a great deal of paperwork and a great deal of paying out, the cottage was mine. Now even at this stage I was not entirely sure that what I wanted in life was a cottage in South Devon. Both Penny and I, after studying our various bank statements, decided on one thing – that, if possible, the cottage must be made to pay for itself in holiday lets. If it didn't we had lumbered ourselves with a thatched millstone.

And, at first, that is what it seemed to be. No, it was more. I was shocked to find that an 'unfit for human habitation' order* had been slapped on the cottage. The local council, quite rightly, do this in all cases where a building which falls below certain standards becomes vacant. But the fact that they were right to do so, insisting that a bathroom and proper kitchen should be in place in the premises, didn't ease our pain one little bit.

I was further shattered to find that the cottage was a 'Listed Building'. A 'Listed Building' is really another name for a preservation order. In effect, it means that you must not change the building because it is of historic interest – or that it is important to the preservation of the appearance of the area that it should not be changed.

Now, I am one hundred per cent in favour of that. It would be criminal to pull down or so alter the façade of Thurlestone Village that the place became a concrete monstrosity. But, at that time, it was one more blow to my peace of mind.

On the one hand, I was now the owner of a building that was unfit for human habitation in its present form – because the only method of having a bath as things were was in a tin bath in front of the range, which also supplied the hot water (though there was a proper flush lavatory in a lean-to at the back of the cottage). And on the other hand I was not allowed to alter the premises due to the fact that, under the Town and Country Planning Act of 1968, the building was 'listed'.

It seemed, in my harassed state, that everyone was against me. How could I put a bathroom and kitchen in – the only cooking facilities were the range in the living room or a primus

*I think the actual words were 'It is below standard, being very dark and badly arranged' and 'any prospective purchaser who is not prepared to bring it up to standard will have a closing order placed on the property'.

stove in the lean-to at the back – if I wasn't allowed to touch the cottage?

With some irritation, I put the problem to the Kingsbridge Rural District Council and received only helpful advice in return – which rather took me by surprise. I don't know why I assumed that Kingsbridge R.D.C. would be obstructive, but they weren't at all. I found myself in the ridiculous position of putting my boxing gloves on and then finding that I had been invited not to a punch-up, but to a party in aid of distressed cottage owners!

Miss Eccles helped me, Mr J. H. Savidge, the Chief Executive Officer helped me and so did Mr J. Fowler, the Deputy Public Health Inspector.

The problem of the various orders on the cottage faded away at the touch of a telephone. Of course the 'unfit for human habitation' order would be lifted immediately I put in a kitchen and bathroom. Of course, the listed building problem could be solved if I put in plans for alteration of the rear of the premises, not the front.

You must remember that I was conducting all this at long range. The job of Managing Editor of the *Evening News* only carries so much holiday with it and I had used up all my allocation for the year – so I could only write letters and use the telephone. Which I did with a will.

At this moment I needed sound advice and I got it from Mr James Ogden of William Beer and Son, the solicitors in Fore Street, Kingsbridge, who had handled with great despatch the many problems over the purchase of the cottage itself. It was James Ogden who suggested that I contact Mr Harry Wingate.

Now Harry Wingate is the sort of man that every distressed cottage owner needs in time of alterations. I talked to him by telephone at his office in H. M. Wingate and Son, Waterloo Place, Duncombe Street, Kingsbridge. To get there, you have to drive up Fore Street and turn right down the one-way system. But I couldn't even do that. I was at the end of a telephone. Even so it was quite obvious that we would have to meet at the cottage so that he could see what I wanted done. So I hurtled down one Friday night, stayed at the cottage and was there on the Saturday morning we had picked for the meeting 'on site'.

I don't know quite what sort of man I expected. Over the phone, his voice had carried a soft Devon burr. I was therefore – because he was a builder – expecting some paint-splashed character to arrive at the cottage door. Harry Wingate was definitely not that. If I remember correctly, he wore a blazer and carried with him such an air of knowledge and authority that Penny and I decided in that moment that everything was going to be all right.

And it was. But it was Harry Wingate who took one look at the problem – the cottage – and, after listening to our ideas, incorporated them into one workable plan. We had two problems. One was where we could fit a bathroom and lavatory into such a tiny structure. The second was providing a proper kitchen.

Obviously our problems were nothing new to Harry Wingate – he must have done more cottage conversions and renovations than any man in South Devon. He agreed immediately with Penny that the small partition wall downstairs, which separated the living room from a space under the stair – a space in which my Uncle Charlie had operated his Primus stove – must come down, and suggested that even though it was not a support wall, it would be a good idea for strengthening the whole structure to put in its place an R.S.J.

You will pardon my innocence, you to whom such things are second nature, but I had never heard of an R.S.J. before. It turned out to be a rolled steel joist, which could more than take the load of the upper floor.

He suggested too that the only place to put in a bathroom and upstairs lavatory was to cut the 'master' bedroom – if anything so small could ever rejoice in such a name – in two and put washbasin, bath and lavatory in under the thatch at the back. He eyed the sagging ceilings and said nothing until pressed. They alarmed him not and I decided not to go any further when he said that they would need cutting away to provide decent headroom.

When he had gone, Penny and I looked at each other and I think we knew that we had found the answer to the most pressing problem. More than that – he had said that he would sort out the plans with the local council and would even draft out the proper application for an Improvement Grant.

Harry Wingate did everything that he said he would. Plans of the alterations arrived – though, if you are claiming a grant, you cannot make a start on any work until all has been approved.

My faith in the people of South Devon – and in particular, of Thurlestone, Kingsbridge and district – had, I hope, never faltered. But now it seemed we had so many people helping us that I felt we might even see the day when 'Just-a-Cottage' would be a joy to behold.

Charles and Elsie Bevell kept an eye on everything. Harry Wingate worked away on the technical side, the Kingsbridge R.D.C. helped where they could, and people in the village like Dora Clark-Thomas, one of the mainstays of the Golf Club, who lived opposite, offered encouragement and practical help, Len Jeffery, who lived next door, was always cheery despite a recent terrible road accident (from which he has fortunately recovered), and his son, Gordon, a master builder if ever there was one, put himself out on numerous occasions . . . in fact the whole village seemed to be on our side, from Mr and Mrs Sherman at the village stores at the top end down to the Rector, John Delve, at the lower end.

Even so, things moved slowly. Not because of any obstruction, but simply because things like Improvement Grants take time. It does not help, I tell you now, if your building is a listed one.

Certain procedures have to be observed. A notice was posted on the cottage door and published in the Kingsbridge Gazette. Charles Bevell immediately sent me a copy. It read:

'KINGSBRIDGE RURAL
DISTRICT COUNCIL

Town and Country Planning Act 1968
Application for listed building consent at
'Just-a-Cottage', Thurlestone

NOTICE IS HEREBY GIVEN that application has been lodged with the above Council for a Listed Building Consent for the demolition and rebuilding at the rear of the above premises.

The earliest known photograph of 'Just-a-Cottage', and probably of Thurlestone village, taken in the very early 1900's. The entrance to the cottage is behind the farthest sitting woman. Donald Ilbert stands with the dog, Hilda Coope is the little girl beside the mare called Belle. Mounted is young John Coope. Holding the bit is Mrs. Coope

Thurlestone in the 1920s. The entrance to 'Just-a-Cottage' is hidden by the large bush

Thurlestone Rock, a landmark since the earliest days of the village's history

Any person may inspect the application and the plans etc. accompanying it at the offices of the Council at the address below during office hours and any person who wishes to make representations relating to the application should do so by writing within 21 days of the date of publication of this notice to the Chief Executive Officer at The Manor House, Kingsbridge.

J. H. SAVIDGE,
Chief Executive Officer

Date: March 2nd, 1971 7422"

It was all very formal and as far as I know no one objected. But I was getting nowhere with my request for an Improvement Grant.

As a matter of fact, I think that Rural District Councils, like Kingsbridge, take a lot of stick over these grants. To hear the talk in pubs, you would think that Councils hand out these grants only to the rich and that every rich person in the world gets one when they could well afford to pay for the work themselves.

It is, of course, wrong that anyone who can well afford to bring a cottage up to a modern standard of hygiene should receive such a grant. But, under the law, anyone is entitled to it. The local Councils have no choice – and if it means that more accommodation is brought up to an acceptable standard, then our attitude should be that you have to take the good with the bad, or the rich with the poor.

Though I don't feel that I have to defend my application for a grant, I would say that at the time I applied, I was so deep in debt due to the actual purchase of the cottage that, unless I had been able to get the grant, the cottage would still be without a bathroom and kitchen. However, if my application for a grant had been refused, I suppose I would have managed somehow.

This is not to say that I did not follow up my application with a fervour that must have strained the patience of all concerned. Because I had a listed building, I hunted the grant to Exeter, to the Devon County Council.

There I found to my dismay that, on 'listed' grounds again, my application had to go to the Department of the Environment in London. Now I was on home ground and pressed in the attack. Finally, the Department surrendered, agreed that it was unnecessary for the Minister to sign it personally, and sent it back stamped for approval.

So I got my grant and work finally started on the cottage. Harry Wingate's men got in there and what Penny and I will always think of as the Days of Dust and Debris began.

We were not there – because of our shortage of holiday time – for most of the work. We were really only able to stand and gape once at what seemed to be a cottage that had been hit by an atom bomb. Harry Wingate's cure for sagging ceilings had turned out to be a power-driven saw, which had cut the ceilings straight and true. But it had deposited on the ground floor the remains not only of centuries of thatching, but also dust which seemed to us to date from the time of Elizabeth the First.

Whether, in fact, the debris was that old, I didn't at that moment know – it just looked it! But what can be said without fear of contradiction is that the muck, murk, dust and debris appalled us, because we had to clean and decorate the cottage. The construction work was completed in July. And – following our policy of making the cottage pay for itself – the first tenant was due at the beginning of August.

Harry Wingate had worked miracles. Tucked in, under the roof, at the rear was a tiny bathroom and lavatory. To cope with the limited space, it was not possible to stand up at the sides of the room. Getting into the bath was a bit of a contortionist's feat, but it was possible to stand upright in front of the washbasin – and shave there. Tall men had to back into the lavatory!

At the rear of the building – in place of the dreadful tin-roofed lean-to – was a proper brick structure housing a modern kitchen. All we had to do with that was to get and fit all the modern appliances that such a kitchen deserved.

The living room, despite the dust, was a joy. Here I should tell you that during the work I had received a phone call from Harry Wingate. He sounded grim. 'I'm afraid we've come across a snag – or rather we've had a bit of an accident.' My heart sank. 'During fixing the joist of the living room, part of the ceiling came down . . .' My yelp of alarm didn't need a telephone to carry it to Kingsbridge.

Harry Wingate's voice went on to say that the ceiling was made up of asbestos sheets nailed up, and that during the work, one of them had to be taken down and this one had pulled the others down. Did I want him to put them all up again?

The question puzzled me, though most of my mind could only visualise great gaping holes and sagging bedroom floors. Then Harry Wingate almost chuckled. Not quite, but almost . . . 'There's a nice set of beams underneath,' he said, 'seems a shame to cover them up again.'

Slowly what he was saying penetrated. Did he mean old beams? He did and explained further that the Victorians did not like things looking cottagey, so they often nailed sheets of board over the beams to cover them up and give a smart flat look to the ceiling.

Tragedy had changed to triumph. No, no, no, of course I didn't want them covered up. 'That's what I thought you'd say,' said Harry – and now he was chuckling – 'so I've had the whole lot taken down anyway!' Things were getting better. Now I had a cottage, a proper cottage with its own old beams. I could hardly wait to see them. And I even forgave Harry Wingate his leg-pull.

I don't know what you visualise when thinking of old beams in a roof – probably the same thing as I did. Great massive timbers, gnarled and twisted, smoke-blackened – the 'Just-a-Cottage' beams were nothing like that. For a start they were thin, about three inches wide by about four inches deep and they ran the length of the cottage from front to back. They ran like tram-lines a foot apart right across the whole ground floor. When we first saw them they were grey with dust, obviously very old and some had a primitive form of decoration on them by a chiselled insert on both sides of the bottom edge. In only two places had they been so rotten that Wingate's men had had to repair them.

I now have to look at old photographs of the interior that I took before any work started to remember how dull the asbestos sheet roof was with its narrow wood slats covering the joins. It is difficult to imagine anyone preferring that type of ceiling to the warmth of the old beams – but then fashions come and go and whatever else the Victorians weren't, they were snobs. Cottage beams obviously came into the vast cocoon of class distinctions that they built around their lives and beams, like the legs on pianos, had to be covered up.

It is difficult, too, now to remember all the work that we asked Harry Wingate to do. He prepared and put in the application for grant, which came to over £1,100*, in December, 1970, but it wasn't until the end of May that the grant – of £448 – was approved.

In June, soon after the Wingate troops went into action, Elsie Bevell wrote to us to say that work had started and 'they have certainly knocked it about'. They had too. I have just been refreshing my memory about all the things that had to be done with the aid of a copy of the grant specification.

I enclose it here for the benefit of those contemplating buying a cottage – or just dreaming of doing so. Remember, when you see all this, that 'Just-a-Cottage' may not have been up to modern standards of living facilities, but it was by no means tumbledown and was a cottage which, until a short time before I bought it, had been occupied happily until his death by my uncle.

Imagine, then, the amount of work that would have to be done to a tumbledown cottage or one in a really bad state of repair. Remember, too, that you don't get your grant money until the work has been completed and, most important, approved. But more of that later.

Proposed Improvements and Repairs
at 'Just-a-Cottage', Thurlestone

1. **Works of Improvement**

Demolish existing lean-to structure at rear and cart away.

Excavate for and lay concrete foundations and build 4″ block cavity walling as detailed on plan.

Provide and fix new 6′ 6″ x 2′ 6″ Door and Frame and 4′ 0¾″ x 3′ 6¼″ high window.

Form new flat roof with 6″ x 2 joists and ¾″ Weyroc decking and clad with 3 layer felting laid by specialist.

*In the end the bill came to almost exactly £1,300.

Lay 4″ concrete floor on 4″ hardcore with polythene sheet D.P.C. membrane.
Provide and fix 1″ Fascia and plastic eaves gutters and R.W.P.
Prepare and render new work inside and outside.
Build in 9″ x 9″ H & M Vent to Food Store.
Excavate for and lay new 4″ drain as shown forming Manhole at corner, connect up 2 – 6″ x 4″ Gullies and W.C.
Form curbs to Gullies etc.
Drain under building to be encased in 6″ concrete.
Construct stud partitions on first floor to form Bathroom.
Clad with plasterboard and skimcoat.
provide and fix new flush H.B. door and lining to Bathroom.
Rearrange doors to Bedrooms as shown.

Plumber

Supply and fix 5 ft. Bath complete with C.P. Taps and waste.
22″ x 16″ Wash Basin complete with C.P. taps and waste.
L/L W.C. Suite.
Fortic Tank and Immersion Heater.
Extend ½″ copper water service and connect up all appliances and sanitary ware.
Provide and fix 42″ x 18″ Sink Unit and Cabinet in Kitchen.
Provide and fix high level cupboard in Kitchen as Food Store.
Remove existing Rayburn, build up opening and install new Fireplace.
P.S. sum £30.
Wiring to new work.
P.S. sum £25.

2. **Repair Works Associated With Improvements**

Include the provisional sums for the following.
Repairs and strengthening of 1st Floor.
P.S. £130.
Take down ceilings.
Fix new 2″ x 2″ joists and plasterboard with skim coat.
P.S. £150.

3. **Other Repair Works**

Re-thatching to rear slope and repair to front.
P.S. £165.
Rewiring to Bedrooms and Living room.
P.S. £30.

As a condition of grant approval, the Kingsbridge R.D.C. added that (a) the fixed window sashes to the front bedrooms should be made opening; (b) we provide and fix a handrail to the staircase; (c) the matchboard partition between bedrooms should be lined with plasterboard; and (d) the front of the thatch should have a 'comb-out' as well as repair.

If you are wondering why my grant of £448 is not half of the total coast (an improvement grant is often about half of what you have to spend), the reason is that the Kingsbridge Rural District Council obviously felt that some of the things I was doing were not necessary to improve the cottage up to the standard they required. They fixed the sum of £899 as 'being the expenses which, in our opinion, are proper to be incurred for the execution of the works specified in the application'. I was glad to get anything – my finances at this state were so parlous that it was only family and friends telling me I would be mad not to go on which, at one stage, stopped me from cancelling the whole project and selling the cottage as it stood. They were right. Now I know I would indeed have been stark raving mad!

Not everything on the application, as shown previously, was finally done. For example, in agreement with the Council the food store was omitted as we were installing a refrigerator.

Penny suggested that a partition should be removed in the living room, and it was. The door into the smaller bedroom was made to open a more convenient way, and our plan for putting the dresser into the hole formed by the removal of the old range, didn't work. It wouldn't fit and now we agree that it would have been a mistake.

Harry Wingate had hopes of finding an old bread oven behind the fireplace recess once the range was removed, but it was not to be. There was nothing of interest there.

At last all the work was finished and I happily sent in my application for payment of the grant, subject of course to the Council's inspection and satisfaction. I needed that money very badly. Harry Wingate had been splendid about not pressing me for money, but he had been so long without that my conscience wouldn't stand much more delay. But Mr J. Fowler, the Deputy Chief Public Health Inspector of the Council, had some different ideas. They were mainly small points, but he was not going to give approval for payment until he was fully satisfied.

The points he raised were quite correct but, now that I was itching to get to work on the cottage, I found this extra delay very irritating. So be warned all you cottage lovers – just because the work is finished it doesn't mean that the grant money comes automatically by return of post.

Mr Fowler's main points were that three treads in the staircase needed repair if people were to go up and down our tiny winding staircase safely, that there appeared to be a leak in the main chimney stack (he pointed out that brown liquid condensation was running down the wall in the chimney opening), that the patching of the thatch at the front still required attention (the back had been fully thatched and was still a golden, wheat straw colour), and that he was not happy about the height of the bathroom ceiling.

Harry Wingate came to the rescue again. He met Mr Fowler on site and sorted out most of the problems. Much to my relief, he found that the chimney stack was not leaking, but that the chimney needed capping. The thatch was patched again, and I took on the job – with the assistance of Gordon Jeffery and his partner, Mike Penwell – of repairing the staircase and sorting out some other minor internal problems.

It was only on the bathroom that Mr Fowler and I could not agree. I said that I was six foot two inches and could stand up in the bathroom. Mr Fowler said he was tall and he could not. I asked if he had tried right in front of the mirror. He said he had and he still couldn't. I asked if he was suggesting that I was a six-foot dwarf and he asked if I thought he was a giraffe.

It was all very good-natured, but it was an argument that could not be solved unless we lifted the roof. Fortunately, Mr Fowler was not prepared to force us to do that and finally the bathroom height scraped by. And the grant was paid.

3. *The Paint Eaters*

Now the cottage had to be decorated. And decorating an old cottage means that you have to double the quantity of paint you would use for the interior of a similar little modern house and even then you will run out before you've finished.

The reason for this is simple. The interior of many old cottages is cob. 'Just-a-Cottage' has a stone exterior, but the stone shell was put round an old cob structure. And there is nothing like cob for absorbing paint. Absorbing is the wrong word – cob gulps emulsion paint down and then almost begs for more.

Faced with the mountain of dust and debris – all the major wreckage had, of course, been removed but it is amazing how much keeps on accumulating as you sweep and wash through, starting from the upstairs, if you have any sense – Penny never despaired. I did. I thought we would never manage to see the end of it.

Sweeping and cleaning in this case included stripping off years' and years' accumulation of wall-papers. Now, this may sound a mammoth task, but in most cases the wall-papers came away easily. The pretty decorated paper that Uncle Charlie had put up in the bedrooms a year or two before he died was holding on to other layers of heavier Victorian papers and under those was something heavier, but so rotted from contact with the cob that the whole thing came away in sheets.

Unfortunately, in place after place it brought down chunks of the cob too. At first Penny and I regarded this with horror, but then realised that as we had intended that the walls should be white emulsion anyway, in some cases where the cob fall was not too bad this slight collapse merely added to the cottagey effect. A smooth surface to a cottage wall, we kept telling each other, would not look right.

In fact the words 'very cottagey' were never far from our lips when sloshing white emulsion into cracks and crannies. I have written earlier that cob absorbs paint at gallons per hour, but cracked cob that is too bad to leave absorbs Polyfilla at the same rate.

It was while doing this cleaning and renovating that we realised how grossly over-furnished the cottage was. In the end we had a count of the number of chairs, apart from the arm-chair-kind, in the cottage and were amazed to find that we were the proud possessors of nineteen. I wish I could say that they were all Chippendale or something like it, but they were not. Just ordinary Victorian household chairs.

Soon we were running an almost daily trip into the second-hand furniture shop in Kingsbridge with items of no use to us strapped on to the roof of the car or poking out of the boot.

We moved one huge wardrobe an inch or two – were amazed at its lightness because it turned out to be matchwood – and then discovered to our horror that we could not get it completely away from the wall. Not surprising really – it was holding up the bedroom ceiling! This is a slight exaggeration, I must confess. What had obviously happened was that the ceiling had subsided slightly and pinned the wardrobe to the floor. The problem was solved with a concerted heave and the scarred ceiling was repaired with copious applications of Polyfilla once again.

I must not mislead you into thinking that the cottage was filled with junk. There were some excellent pieces. Not classic furniture of any great value, but some made by local craftsmen – in particular, the great dresser in the living room which had been a wedding present to my aunt and uncle. But there was far too much of it. You really couldn't move for furniture.

Gradually we got the cottage under control. The walls whitened. We gave the outside walls a coat of white emulsion too, and panicked Gordon Jeffery into doing the same for his father's cottage, right next door. Len Jeffery welcomed our efforts – our white did make his look grey for a while until Gordon moved in – because, said Len, his son was always being called out to do other people's building jobs and never had time for work closer to home! I have heard Gordon's wife, June, make the same complaint!

We fell into bed each night, arms aching from paint-brushes, exhausted in our race to get the cottage ready for our first tenants. And as we got more and more tired of the work, we would switch from outside to inside in an effort to break the monotony of some of the jobs.

It sounds silly, really that we found so much work to do when you know how tiny the cottage is. But we were really starting from scratch.

In my uncle's time the cottage had been a dull olive green on the outside. Having had some experience with yacht paint on our house in London, we determined that the cottage should be the same gay blue and that it would be coated with the same yacht paint. Our interest in a paint designed for yachts stemmed from our interest in boating and seeing our own boat's paintwork stand up to incredibly hard wear. If the paint could take the sort of bashing it got in a boat, we argued, then it should last even longer on a house.

Our house in London had proved this to our lazy satisfaction. It lasted longer, held its colour and seemed much more weather-resistant than the normal paints designed for house exteriors. So 'Just-a-Cottage' got its coat of sparkling blue. Looking back at the cottage on our way down to the village pub for a bit of relaxation in the early evening, I must confess I was pleased with what we had done. The cottage walls sparkled washing-powder white in the late sunlight and the blue seemed totally in keeping with the village atmosphere.

But there really wasn't all that much work on the outside, and duty drove us back in again once the outside was finished. Inside, it was a different matter. There, problem after problem confronted us. I don't think you can ever finish improving a cottage. Even when all the basic decoration has been done to your satisfaction, you will see in a shop just the thing to complete the picture – and then something else. . . .

It was all very boring for our children – holidays in a child's world depend on activity and frequent changes of scene. But we used them shamelessly. Once the walls were whitened – and pronounced 'very cottagey' – with Kevin and Joanna going round and round on 'touch-up' missions, we were still missing such vital things as floor-coverings, light-fittings, and beds for the smallest bedroom. But before we could even think about things like that we had to cope with the beams.

Now, beams are beams. And beams should look, you will agree, like beams. They should be dark, reflecting the candlelight on the polished table, rapiers, the flushed cheeks of pretty ladies, and ancient brass. Well, you know what I mean. . . .

The trouble with our beams was that, even when cleaned of the dust, they remained obstinately greyish-brown. We went into Kingsbridge with our problem. If you don't know Kingsbridge, let me enlighten you a little. Fore Street winds steeply up from the quay. It takes a lot of traffic, but it is also the heart of the town. Here, you either have to gamble on finding a parking spot on its steep sides, or park on the quay at the bottom and walk up. Or you can park in the town park at the top and walk down. Either way you will find that unless you plan your shopping expedition with great care and local knowledge, you will find yourself at the top of Fore Street with your car parked up there and the last item on your list is in a shop right at the bottom. Or vice-versa.

Despite this, Kingsbridge is a great town. Everything you need is in that street or one of the little side streets down on the flat. I am serious about this – it is a splendid shopping centre. The only thing for which I have found the town wanting is that if you want to have a key copied – a common need of all who let their cottages to pay the mortgage (and there are more of us than would care to admit it) – then you have to go elsewhere. If such facilities exist by the time this book has been published, then those concerned will just have to forgive me.

I have digressed. We were talking about beams. Our beams. Our obstinately grey-brown beams. Kingsbridge not only supplied the answer, but also the materials. You would think that they have been dyeing beams for centuries. Perhaps they have. But, anyway, we soon found ourselves applying a dark stain of incredible stickiness to our beams.

I think this was the straw that nearly broke the decorators' backs. If you have never done it, you will have no idea of how painting a beam with dye means an almost total surrender to being coated with dye yourself. It means that your arms ache, and though the beam absorbs the stain to the manner born, it also runs down your brush, down your fingers, down your arms and ends up not only in your armpit but also on your knees and feet!

The time of our beam-staining coincided with more than

the usual Thurlestone fine weather – a heatwave. We painted and we dried and we were black all down one side! And when that was finally done, we still had the real decoration of the cottage to do. We had to put the gilt on the gingerbread.

You may be amazed at our panic rush to meet our first holiday-maker's deadline. But we needed the money. Wingate needed the money. He never said a word, but fair is fair. And, despite the grant money, we still owed him a deal of pounds. We swapped furniture at the second-hand furniture store in Kingsbridge, as cottage-owners in the area have been doing for years, in order to get the cottage into letting order.

Away went the big double bed. In its place we put the single bed from the smaller bedroom and added one. That sorted out the main bedroom – I will not joke by calling it the 'master bedroom' again, as one local owner did about a room even smaller than the one we were offering!

The small bedroom, however, was a real source of worry to us. It was, and is, so tiny that the only way of providing accommodation for two people is by the use of bunk beds. But bunk beds cost a lot of money, and second-hand ones, we found, were just not available.

It was at this moment that Penny and I knew that we needed a break. The cottage had become an obsession and we badly needed a change of scene. Such a change was exactly seventeen miles away, close to Plymouth, and devoted to one of our major interests in life.

The place we were both thinking about was Fort Bovisand, which was an old Napoleonic fort designed to defend Plymouth against a French invasion, and which has now been converted into the best centre for underwater sport in Britain. This conversion, which makes our work on the cottage look pretty miniscule, meant changing a great barracks of a place with huge gun casemates into a place where aqualung divers could stay, get everything they need to continue their sport – and, most important, where they could do all these things in comfort. As keen divers and members of the British Sub-Aqua Club ourselves, we rate Fort Bovisand very highly.

Looking at the vast amount of work that Alan Bax and Jim Gill had done – it includes, by the way, one of the best bars in England, with a view from panoramic windows over the whole of Plymouth Sound – I think both Penny and I felt pretty junior members of the Devon conversionists association!

Alan and Jim showed us over what they had done – to my mind, a non-technical, all fingers and thumbs man, it ranks with the Seven Wonders of the World and if you have the chance of going there, don't miss it. During the course of our guided tour, one of them told us that the bunk beds we saw there in abundance came from a war-surplus store – a real war-surplus store (none of your manufactured goods specially for war-surplus sale!) – down in Plymouth Docks.

I can't tell you how good this store is – it is worth a visit even if you have no bunk beds in mind. We bought cheaply a set of Admiralty (sailors, for the use of) bunk beds and since then we have brought boat covers, binoculars, thermos outfits . . . in fact, our difficulty is getting away *without* buying anything. The staff are incredibly helpful and even searched great boxes of assorted keys for me on one occasion when I couldn't get copies made quickly for a lock on the cottage door.

Those Admiralty bunks fitted into the small bedroom as though the Navy had us in mind when they made them. The only trouble with them was that they did need a bit of a climb to get into the top berth. But they have gone now – we were able to buy a more luxurious set from someone in the village who had decided that she no longer wanted to play the letting game.

The next problem was the floors. We had to buy expensive modern equivalents of lino to cover them, having found to our amazement that lino was not made any more, or if it was, that the big stores in Plymouth no longer stocked it. They sent us, with toffee-nosed disapproval, to some little corner shop on the road to Cornwall, but lino was obviously out. So we paid a small fortune for something more modern. The fact is, of course, that though it looked better, as soon as we were really in the letting business, it was torn every time tenants moved the furniture.

The floor and the furniture were now there. But I wanted the cottage interior to be particularly 'Thurlestone'.

So I got the *Evening News* Art Department to copy – and renovate – old photographs of Thurlestone as it was in the

1800's. I then put them into old frames that we had found in the cottage some time before. Those pictures are there now and they do give, I think, some idea of the village life of long ago.

One thing I did learn, as I put these pictures up on the walls, was that cob is no place to hang anything. The truth is that if you put an ordinary nail into a cob wall, it just disappears. I am not joking when I say that you need a nail at least six inches long to get a grip in the heart of the cob. And even that may not be long enough.

Though we were scared of cob collapses – whole walls in well-looked-after cottages can suddenly decide to give way without any warning, as you will see from the picture facing page 65 of a collapsed wall at 'Woodbine' when my mother owned it – it did work to our advantage by the front downstairs window. While we were painting, I noticed that the top one of two shelves there was decidedly wobbly. In fact, so wobbly was it, that it had to come down. No amount of Pollyfilla would cope with such a structural weakness. It only needed the slightest of tugs and, as a disturbing small avalanche of cob fragments rattled to the floor, away it came. Only when this top shelf had gone did we realise that we were looking at a window seat. The top shelf had completely masked the real purpose of the wider lower shelf.

A small discovery, but it was this sort of thing which made fitting out the cottage so interesting. Back and forth we went between Thurlestone and Kingsbridge. The electric cooker arrived, the fridge arrived. We hung mirrors, fixed lights, got mattresses to fit the beds, arranged the table so that the window seat was one of the sitting places, put the chairs around it, touched up places on beams or walls that we had missed, and then finally decided we could do no more. Everything worked – and the immersion heater provided hot water at such a rate that we were finally able to soak all the paint off us.

We knew even then that we still had a great deal more to do to the cottage before it would be just the way we wanted it, but time had beaten us now. So on the Friday afternoon we locked the front door, handed over the keys to Elsie and Charles Bevell, who had agreed to look after it during the time it was let, and set off for Cornwall for a week's rest.

It was funny to think of someone coming into that cottage

the next day to make it their holiday home for the next few weeks. We felt a twinge of envy. We felt it even more later. The sun had shone all the time we had worked on the cottage in Thurlestone; in Cornwall for our holiday it poured with rain!

We wondered how our first tenants had got on. Had we forgotten something vital? And then, out of the blue, came a letter from Seale, near Farnham in Surrey. It began: 'As we have been your first holiday tenants we thought you might be interested in our reactions to a three-week stay.

'Firstly, we have enjoyed our stay sufficiently to book again for next year. . . .' The letter was signed 'P.R. Knowles' and Mr Knowles took the cottage each year until he finally got a place of his own. He wrote that nice letter correctly guessing that we really wanted to know how he had reacted. He made several suggestions for small improvements in the letter and we were only too glad to act on them.

One thing that we did know was needed if we were to continue in the letting business was parking space. Thurlestone Village is not wide enough for all day parking outside each cottage door, particularly at the spot where 'Just a Cottage' and 'Home Cottage' are sited, almost opposite the corner of the turning that leads to Buckland and Bantham. People parking right outside his door had infuriated my Uncle Charlie so much that he had even gone to the trouble of making his own 'No Parking' sign. This he would stick in the earth of the tiny patch in front of the cottage which could never, by any stretch of imagination, be called a front garden.

It is particularly because that front door opens almost directly on to the street that you do not want other people's cars parked within touching distance of your front windows. Even your own is a nuisance there.

So we needed a parking space. There was, of course, only one place for it – in the back garden of 'Just-a-Cottage', which is separated from the house, although we have, of course, the right of way along a leafy path to it and the right of access by car to the garden down a private road. This road also enables the owners of 'Woodbine' – Brigadier Simon and Mrs Terry Gavourin to get their cars into their garage, which is the present function of the little cottage inside which my grandfather used to keep his rough cider casks.

The simplest thing to do would be to put up a garage on the end of my garden in place of the greenhouse. Or so I thought. Until I looked at that greenhouse. Have you ever seen a greenhouse with walls nearly two foot thick? To knock it down or convert it to a garage would be a major operation. Who could have built such a greenhouse in the first place? The explanation from one of the older inhabitants of the village was simply that the building had never started out in life as a greenhouse at all. In fact, it had been pig-pens. Mighty stout pig pens, but quite clearly that was what had happened. A stout Devon pig-pen had been converted into a greenhouse and, knowing my uncle's delight in gardening, I am sure that he did the conversion.

If knocking down the piggery-greenhouse was not on, what could I do? It blocked the way to the garden as far as a car was concerned as surely as a concrete Army pillbox would block an armoured car.

The way round it was simply that – round it. So after a bit of friendly negotiations with Arthur Stidston, who owns that private road, he agreed to let me have a courtesy right to use a further twenty-one feet of his road beyond my rights of access for the huge sum of £1 per year.

We both gained. I was now able to take down some feet of hedge to get into my future parking place and he, as a result of my removal of the hedge, did not have tall saplings blocking his view of the sea.

And it would make letting the cottage much easier for Joy Tompkins, who handled our holiday tenants from her office in Fore Street, Kingsbridge. A keen golfer, she travels regularly to play on the wonderful Thurlestone course and knows only too well how cars parked outside the cottages can block the narrow village street.

This was all right so far, but my parking place did not exist and was occupied at that moment by two tumbledown sheds and a patch of the best weeds in Devon. The sheds had been used as a dumping ground for anything unwanted since my grandfather's day. So our next holiday was earmarked for tearing down the sheds and investigating the contents.

4. *The Secrets of the Sheds*

As soon as we started work on the destruction of the sheds, we stepped back into another world. The world of Victoriana.

My elder sister, Christine, loves old things and to have left her out of the exploration of the sheds would have been a needless act of cruelty. So she came down with us to the cottage. In fact, any extra help was, I felt, going to be very useful. Those sheds looked very much embedded into the ground.

Most of the contents were junk. There were bits of old beds, old planks, even an old G.P.O. bicycle, which had seized solid long ago. The sun shone and there was no wind to carry sparks to nearby thatch so we started a fire to destroy old worm-eaten boxes. The sun got hotter and hotter and so did the fire, and soon sweat was running in great streaks through the grime on our faces.

For a while we seemed to be getting nowhere – the insides of the sheds were piled up to the rotting roofs with material that I doubted had been worth saving at the time it was dumped inside. But we gradually worked our way through. And old chests started appearing. It was then that I suddenly found myself working alone and Penny and Christine were strangely quiet. I went round to the side of the shed away from the fire. They had discovered what to them was obviously a treasure house. One of the chests was open between them and they kept diving in with small squeaks of delight.

The contents were obviously my grandmother's. Each packet of tissue paper unwrapped produced a brand-new long skirt, or nightdress or one of those long chemises that I presume Victorian ladies wore underneath all those long dresses. There was even a proper whalebone corset and then small boxes of jet jewellery, mourning jewellery undoubtedly. And though it could have been of the kind worn by the Victorians to join Victoria in her mourning for Albert, I thought immediately of all those little framed black-edged cards for children my grandmother had borne, but who had not survived.

There were other cards of buttons and cards of lace and some of the skirts even had the price on them still – one at one shilling and ninepence seemed very good value (Penny has worn it at informal dinner parties since then and still has it and others from the same chest). In most cases these clothes stood up to washing and some of the lace came up as good as new. Some, of course, just fell to pieces.

Other chests contained small amounts of goodies, such as gold pins for my grandfather's ties or cravats, and the beautiful and ornate combs that went with those upswept Victorian hair-styles.

The sharp combs themselves could be a hazard. I remember my mother telling me how she cut herself badly when sneaking in late one night. Apparently, she slipped and bumped her head just where the comb was and fearful of discovery crept into bed and finally despite her aching head fell asleep. Only to be woken in the morning by her mother's screams when she found her daughter in bed asleep on a pillow which was smothered in blood!

Among this sort of thing there were other items like picture frames, which Christine pounced on joyfully. They would do well for the walls of her dream cottage when she got it (they are on the walls of her home, Holly Cottage in Sturminster Marshall, today, so she was not looking so far ahead after all!).

So the fire went on growing and there were long intervals between feeding it when we found anything interesting. Three items pleased me very much. First, my grandfather's travelling chest came to light. Looking just like a sea-captain's chest with bow top, it had runners in the base for ease of handling. It was boldly labelled 'W. K. Hill New York' and it was the one he took with him when he left Plymouth as a young man and sailed for the United States. He tried to join the police force there – his uncle was a police inspector in Devon – but failed. Nor did he get any sort of decent job, though he even tried to become a tram driver. In the chest too was a magnificent American Bible, complete with clasp and lock, which had been given to him by some young lady over there. I fancy he was a bit of a lad in his day!

The chest, revarnished, now occupies pride of place in the

cottage living room in the alcove where the big iron range used to be.

The other things we found in the shed which I liked very much were two metal Victorian hat boxes. These were rusted, but not badly so, and I could see that with a coat of paint over some rust-killing undercoat they could be very handsome items indeed. When we had finished work on them, we stencilled on the initials 'W.P.B. and that is what they now are in the cottage – upstairs and downstairs wastepaper baskets.

Soon we had emptied one of the sheds and consigned the shell of it to the flames. Then we started on the second. If we had hoped for a similar treasure trove we were greatly disappointed. This really was a gardening shed and except for some handsomely decorated old beer bottles, which are in the cottage today, the contents were much more ordinary, mostly rotten old gardening tools and packets of rusting nails.

This shed, as it was mostly made of corrugated iron cemented into a concrete base was much more difficult to move and break up, but we finally managed it. The area was cleared as well as we could do it. The next step was for a bull-dozer to come in and flatten the ground ready for an application of gravel chippings. After all our hard work we expected it to be done quickly, but in fact it took nearly a year to get the parking place into satisfactory order. Until then, everyone's car got stuck on the sloping bare earth.

As I have said before, our problem with the cottage was not that it didn't have enough furniture, but rather that it had too much. I got quite a thing about renovating the old chests we had found in the sheds and there are at least three in the cottage today. Stripped, varnished and with brass handles added they are, I think, splendid and certainly 'very cottagey'! As my chests moved in some of the chairs had to move out.

We sold one or two items that were of no sentimental value to us, such as one or two Victorian clothes and the odd tie-pin. This brought us into contact with the world of antique shops. We found some amusement when we discovered quite accidentally that there are certain trigger-phrases that send antique-dealers into a screaming tizzy of anxiety. And certain automatic responses they make when you are the seller.

You shouldn't take this as a guide on how to beat the

antique-dealer at his own game – but it might give you a few ideas. I should add that anything which follows refers to London dealers, so you see we were jumping in at the deep end!

First, the trigger-phrases that ensure not only the dealer's instant attention, but also a better price for anything you have to sell. Try these:

'I've just bought an old cottage and it seems to be full of junk, is this worth anything?' (You should then produce something of reasonable value to back up your words.)

'I'm sorry to bother you, but I've just acquired an old cottage in Devon and it's got so much furniture in it, you can hardly turn round. . . .'

'I've just been going through my grandfather's things in an old cottage he left me, and I wondered. . . .'

You may laugh, but I am not joking. After saying something similar to one of the above, I have had antique-dealers offering to drive their vans all the way down to South Devon that very night so that they could give me 'a proper valuation'. One antique-dealer gave me £5 for two calico Victorian slips so that I would be softened up enough to give him the 'exclusive rights' to look at the rest of the contents of the cottage.

You cannot blame them I suppose. The combination of the words 'cottage' and 'furniture' seems to drive even the hardest into the word 'greed' almost at once. The reason is, I suspect, that somewhere in the antique-dealer's book of legends is the story of the dealer who took a look inside a cottage offered to him by some innocent and bought the contents outright for a fiver. This legendary dealer is now sunning himself in his own cottage in the South of France ('It was all Chippendale, old boy.') and has never had to work again – or so the story will go.

I suppose I shouldn't be unkind. It wouldn't be much of a dealer who didn't react to the chance of raping a virgin cottage, now would it?

And if you think I am unkind, then perhaps it is because I have seen the other side too. The dealer who tells you that your old bowl is no good because it should have been (a) thicker, (b) thinner or (c) because it has a crack (despite the fact that all he has on offer are bowls with similar slight defects). My advice in such a circumstance is to take your goods away immediately. You will be able to tell by his reaction whether he was trying it on. Never, never, never, take a low price for any of the above reasons.

I speak from experience. The only item worth anything among the huge amount of crockery in the cottage was a piece that I thought came from Woolworth's. Fortunately, because I saw a similar piece in an antique shop window, I was able to rescue it from the pile being taken to the dustbin. But even so, the price I was given for it was nothing like the price of similar bowls on display. It was a piece of lustreware and some imagined flaw brought the price down to almost nothing. Foolishly I accepted. I am bitter about it, not because I liked it – on the contrary I thought it ugly and still do – but because I was taken for a ride. I saw the same piece some weeks later on display in the same antique shop – damned cheek! – for five times what I accepted for it. And it disappeared, so presumably it was sold at that price.

I can now see every antique-dealer reader rising in wrath about the things I have said. So, if it will make them happier, I will tell you a story about the contents of the cottage which shows how every amateur thinks everything of his is worth a fortune.

I have told you how we turned out the sheds. In them – in ghastly frames – were some rather nice prints. I liked them and brought them back to town for framing in the same style as all the old photographs I wanted on the cottage walls.

The prints were nice, but I knew nothing about them. They bore the mark of a man called George Baxter. I mentioned casually to a friend that I had some prints by a man called Baxter and he did an antique-dealer on me. He thought they were of great value and did some research. When he gave me this information I thought my fortune was made:

'George Baxter was born in Lewes, Sussex in 1804, and was the son of a well-known printer and publisher. He became an engraver in 1827 in the Blackfriars Road and experimented with colour printing. By 1835, he had perfected his process and patented it. His works originally appeared in books and then as separate prints. His prints are rare.'

I knew it! I had liked those prints from the very start! One showed a family preparing to emigrate and the other showed them already there. I rang Sotheby's and was put through to their fine arts section. I described the prints and waited for an instant summons to bring them along. What sort of reserve had I got in mind? – that was the next sort of question I expected.

Instead a very knowledgeable voice asked me more about the prints and then almost audibly sighed. 'They're nice,' he said, 'but what a pity they are those particular ones. He turned out thousands for the Great Exhibition of 1851. I'd say they were worth about a fiver.'

Just my luck. Of all the examples to get hold of, I have to find the only ones that Baxter turned out in quantity. Oh, well, I thought, easy come, easy go – and in my heart I suppose I had never really believed that they were worth a fortune. Or so I tell myself now! So you see the contents of the cottage and of the sheds were really more decorative than anything else.

If by these stories of the early days of our occupation of 'Just-a-Cottage' I have put you off your family heirlooms, then you must forgive me. The real price of anything old is the value you put on it. Every cottage owner will agree with me when I say that it is the possession of something with a history, something old that you can dream about and something which no one can copy today – that is the true value of an old cottage.

5. *Detective Work*

Finding out about your cottage is fun. People who would not pass any time of day in a churchyard, would not dream of ploughing through old newspaper files, would not spend ten minutes in a public library, and certainly would go nowhere near the British Museum or Public Record Office, have been known to devote hours of time they would normally call precious, searching out facts about a tiny square of land occupied by an old building.

So you will not be surprised to find that I have devoted some of my energies to trying to find out the history of the stones under the thatched roof which is now called 'Just-a-Cottage'.

One thing is certain. I can tell you here and now that it was not called 'Just-a-Cottage' until 1931. I say that with complete certainty because on the day that my grandfather made over the cottage to his son, Charlie, the conveyance states quite clearly that the Vendor conveyed to the Purchaser 'all that freehold cottage and premises situate immediately in front of the back premises known as Woodbine Cottage in the Parish and Village of Thurlestone'. And if the cottage had been known then as 'Just-a-Cottage' it would have been so described.

So we are left with an un-named cottage on the main street of Thurlestone. Un-named, that is, prior to 1931. So now the detective story starts. Every detective story needs a few clues, so here we go, right back to early history.

One can only suspect that Thurlestone was part of the land trodden by Iron Age warriors. But it is a pretty good guess because high up on Bolt Tail, overlooking Inner Hope and the whole of Bigbury Bay, is an Iron Age fort.

The fort is there today, preserved by the National Trust land on which it stands. Across the promontory those Iron Age people threw up a rampart over 800 feet long and nearly ten feet high. It was no simple affair and was complete with outstations and a twisty entrance. It had its own fresh-water supply and was ideally situated to keep an eye on Hope Cove far below.

Archaeologists will probably correct me but I would have thought that such a fort implied, either a fear of attack from the sea, or supply from the sea. And either reason means that the shipping along the coast was great enough to want to defend or protect a natural harbour like Hope.

So we can assume that in Iron Age days there was a fair amount of activity at sea in the Thurlestone area. I think one tends to forget in these days of big, big ships, which rarely come inshore, how much the Thurlestone area depended on the sea; just as today a visitor would be amazed to know that fishing for pilchards in the 1800's was such a thriving industry that they were even sold abroad.

We are digressing from ancient history, but it is important, I think, that in considering the past, one should know that pilchard fishing from small boats in the area in the last century was so big that one record catch was estimated at 2,000,000 fish. The fish were caught – following the sighting of the shoals from the top of Burgh Island – by small boats drawing their nets around the shoal and were then cured at Bigbury and Challaborough or Bantham. All that is gone now, of course. Times change, fish change their habits, but it is the sort of sudden disappearance of local industry that in very ancient times would have left little, if any, trace.

So we do not know the reason for the Iron Age fort being abandoned. Perhaps the fish left, perhaps the fort was overwhelmed, perhaps the Iron Age got left behind by the times.

Be that as it may, the next evidence I can find of activity in the area is written, for Thurlestone appears in the Domesday Book. The reason for the book was simply that William the Conqueror during the period from 1068 to 1071 needed to check on the amount each area should pay to the Crown.

So we find in the Exeter Domesday Book this sort of thing: 'Juhel has a manor called Torlestan which John held T.R.E. and it paid geld for 2 hides. These six ploughs can till. . . .

'There Juhel has 15 villeins, 6 bordars, 4 cottagers, 5 serfs, 1 rouncey, 16 swine, 150 sheep, 2 acres of meadow and 2 acres of pasture. Worth 60 shillings; when Juhel received it 4 pounds.'

T.R.E. is not an abbreviation for the Thurlestone Royal

Engineers, but a quick way of writing 'Tempore Regis Edwardi', literally 'on the day King Edward was alive and dead', in other words the day he died.

Juhel seems to have played an important part in William the Conqueror's campaigns. The Domesday Book was compiled in 1068 and was first published in readable English in 1783. A 'hide' was something in the region of one hundred acres and the reference to 'six ploughs' was an estimate of the amount of tillable land. A villein was a tenant farmer; a bordar, a craftsman; and a rouncey is so delightful that I hesitate to find out!

Juhel seems to have supported the wrong side in the problems over succession which followed William the Conqueror's death. He supported Robert when he should have supported Rufus, who succeeded. So Rufus, obviously peeved, took Thurlestone away from Juhel and gave it to Rogerius, who already owned much land in Normandy.

I have not room here to go into the various early owners of Thurlestone, but it is interesting to note that in 1274 Edward the First had a commission to inquire into everyone who claimed royal rights in Britain. The lords of Thurlestone did not appear, but sent an attorney to represent them at the court. And the attorney said that they claimed to have the right to inspect gallows, bread and ale made in Thurlestone and 'free warren on their own manor lands there without license'. The attorney was appearing on behalf of Hugh de Ferrars and his wife, Alice.

Though the Latin does not specifically say that it existed, the idea of a gallows actually at Thurlestone is disturbing. But there probably was such a thing to enforce the rights of the lord of the manor, who had the power to inflict death by hanging.

Later on – in 1346 – John de Chevereston held Thurlestone manor and the manor of Ilton, and this leads us into one of the most famous families in the area, for John de Chevereston settled the manor of Thurlestone on his father-in-law, Hugh Courtenay, Earl of Devon. The Courtenays held Thurlestone until 1869.

We have travelled fast through the centuries – and barbaric ones they were, too. For example, in 1328, blood was shed in Thurlestone Church, and the Abbot of Buckfast had to 'reconcile' the parish church before it could be used for services again.

The parishioners had to pay special dues for this reconciliation and if they did not they were liable to be excommunicated. We don't know what the bloodshed in the church was, but it was probably a murder, as a small affray would hardly have called for such special services.

Just prior to the Civil War the Thurlestone living fell vacant because the parish priest was caught selling his services – offering to cure souls for money – and was therefore guilty of the sin 'Simony', named after Simon Magus who offered money to St Peter in exchange for spiritual powers.

The man who took on the living was a warlike rector indeed. His name was John Snell. And John Snell, with the on-set of the Civil War, had no doubt where his duties lay – he was all for King and country. So were the local gentry and they fortified the ruins of King Henry VIII's old castle, which had guarded the entrance to the Salcombe Estuary. The 'Old Bullworke' they called it then, and bulwark for the Royalists it turned out to be. Half a dozen Thurlestone men were among the new garrison behind the hastily-strengthened walls. And who do you think was the chaplain of Salcombe Castle? Right – none other than the Rector of Thurlestone, John Snell.

For a while the Castle seems to have served as a protection for Royalist privateers using Salcombe Harbour as a base. It was twice attacked from the sea but beat off both attacks – any yachtsman today will tell you that it is in a tricky corner if the winds are wrong. The ruins today still have a certain grandeur.

But the Parliamentarians captured both Dartmouth and Plymouth and poor old Salcombe Castle was all on its own. The garrison still appears to have controlled the entrance from the sea and there is more than a suggestion that a great chain across the Estuary entrance stopped all traffic until the later days of the siege.

Because siege there was. The Castle held out – the last place in Devonshire to stand for the King – for four months, from January to May of 1646. When it finally surrendered the garrison was accorded all the honours of war. They came out with drums beating and colours flying and only handed over their arms when they reached East Allington – and then they were free to go.

One of the articles in the surrender arrangements was that John Snell should be allowed to return to his parsonage in Thurlestone and there live in peace. But it didn't happen like that. His cattle and household goods were plundered and he had to fly for his life. But he survived to return to his living at the Restoration of Charles II and was rewarded for his troubles by being made Canon of the Cathedral Church of St Peter, Exeter.

After the return of Charles II Thurlestone had to provide ten foot-soldiers and a mounted man for the militia, the equivalent of today's Territorials.

And talking of that sort of Army, Mr Frank Coope reveals in his splendid booklet* that in the summer of 1803, the volunteer artillery, camped on Malborough Down, amused themselves by firing at Thurlestone Rock! But does not record, because he could not find out, whether they hit it or not.

What has all this to do with the age of a cottage in Thurlestone? The answer is – everything. For if you do not know the history of the area in which your cottage is sited, you are wasting your time in a lot of your searches.

I know that I have raced you through the history of Thurlestone pulling out highlights that are of interest to everyone, but every clue is of help in dating a cottage. It is a lucky man who finds his cottage with the date of completion right above the door. Some do have such luck, of course, and some builders have been proud enough to have not only the date but also their name inscribed on a tablet let into the wall.

During my search to find the date of 'Just-a-Cottage' I have consulted source after source. Which is why when invited to spend a weekend with friends, Evelyn and Leslie Kark of Lucie Clayton model agency fame, I looked with something close to black jealousy at the stone let in above the entrance to their Cotswold retreat in Burford. There, as clear as anything, is the date — 1696. Now why couldn't the builder of 'Just-a-Cottage' have been just as thoughtful!

One of my problems in dating the cottage is the shortage of records concerning the village itself. The records of the church, on the other hand, which are now in the Devon Record Office

**Thurlestone Church and Parish* by the Reverend Frank Egerton Coope, M.A., who was Rector of Thurlestone from 1897 to 1921.

in South Street, Exeter, are fairly full. This is understandable – the parish priest would have been the most educated man in the area, but naturally he was concerned almost totally with records of the church and not with making notes about the cottages in the village. There are odd references which are useful but they are not specific enough to help me.

There was a church on the present site early in the thirteenth century, possibly even the twelfth. Throughout the ages the church catered for a mainly agricultural community. The Church registers date from 1558.

The discovery of which I dream is an old map of the village, prior to the sixteenth century, showing each house in its place, but I am afraid such a thing does not exist. The earliest map with any detail upon it seems to be the Tithe Map of about 1840. The Tithe Map surveyed every field, house, garden – in fact, every piece of property in the area.

When the map was complete every plot was given a number, and you have only to look up the number in the Tithe Apportionment Book, which goes with the map, to find out the owner, the occupier, the acreage, the land use, and the tithe rent claimed on it. This tithe went to the upkeep of the parish priest.

So, if I couldn't at the moment prove any earlier date, at least I could be sure that my cottage was in existence in 1840. I then wrote to the Devon Record Office. Had they got the Thurlestone Tithe Map of 1840? Yes, they had – could I give them a precise reference so that they could track down my cottage?

I could and did. But back came a most disappointing letter from Mr P. A. Kennedy, the County Archivist.

He wrote: 'I am afraid we are unable to assist you with details of "Just-a-Cottage" from the Tithe Map. Unfortunately the map has been rubbed in places, and the number on your plot is quite undecipherable. It appears that a house stood there at the time, but it is not possible to tell the exact size, owing to the condition of the map.'

Just my luck. But never mind. At least the house was there at the time. So it must be earlier than 1836 when the survey was done for the 1840 map.

I went on asking for help. Letters flew this way and that. The Reverend John Delve, the present Rector of Thurlestone, pointed out a gift of glebe land for the building of Thurlestone's Church House on June 16th, 1536, but was forced to add that he didn't think the glebe extended as far as my cottage.

Mr Fowler of Kingsbridge Rural District Council, with whom I had battled over the payment of my grant, helped again with a suggestion that Mr W. R. Grose, of The Swallows, Thurlestone, would be worth asking as he was writing a history of the Thurlestone Hotel.

The Groses are a well-known Thurlestone family – they own the luxurious Thurlestone Hotel, and, until recently, owned the Links Hotel, down by Leas Foot, as well. So, as I wasn't able to get down to the cottage at the time, I wrote to Mr Grose, whom I remember meeting as a boy. I should have thought of this before as the Thurlestone Hotel own the cottage next door to mine which they rent to Leonard Jeffery and his wife.

Mr Grose wrote back an encouraging letter: 'I am afraid I have no direct evidence as to the age of the cottages. At the moment one can only hazard a guess from the type of construction and the materials used. I have an idea (but no evidence) that at one time Leonard's cottage and yours were one house and that would put the date about the 16th century.

'Leonard's cottage was, at one time, two and we put them into one without drastic alteration of the interior.

'If the interior walls were found not to be tied to the exterior, that would be evidence of late division, possibly under the Puritans. This was found to be the case with Church House when it was repaired by the local Council. . . .'

Mr Grose had put into words a thought that had been somewhere in the back of my mind for a long time. It had always struck me as being odd that anyone should build such a tiny cottage as 'Just-a-Cottage'. However, with the thought of my cottage and Leonard Jeffery's as one building, not the three cottages of recent years, a very different picture of the whole thing emerged. Then the building would have been worth putting up as a full-sized house.

I could not, however, without drastic measures, such as pulling something down, find out if the interior walls were tied or not. So the question raised by Mr Grose of Puritan division will have to wait for a while.

You can, of course, guess a great deal about the age from the way the cottage was built. And here I may have a vital clue. The oldest kind of cottage is one where basic tree trunks have been used for the frame and the spaces in between have been filled in with wattle and daub and then plastered. Stone was in short supply and so were masons. In fact, it was not until the sixteenth century that stone was used to any great extent and then it was often used to cover and strengthen existing homes.

Now, 'Just-a-Cottage' could be one of those, and there are two reasons why I say that. Firstly, the interior walls are of cob. Secondly, the exterior walls are of stone. So at some time or other someone thought it worth covering the cottage as it was then with a stone facing. Cob is really a mud pie of straw, clay, cow-dung, anything of the kind that was handy locally and was used in the earliest days of country building.

The cottage has a cob interior, there is no doubt about that – just try hanging a picture! But when Harry Wingate and I were looking at the cottage, prior to the alterations, he pointed out to me that some of the exterior stones had been removed where the lean-to was attached to the back of the cottage and behind them was an exposed portion of the material behind the wall. As we looked up at it I was amazed to see strips of what looked like young saplings woven through a sort of brown crust. Wattle and daub! So the cottage could be sixteenth century – or it could be even older than that.

It is easy, of course, if you are an amateur detective, to let your imagination race ahead of the facts. In fact, I am at the moment letting a wild idea race around in my day-dreams. Supposing that the cottage and Leonard Jeffery's two-in-one cottage were all one in the 1500's. That would make it a sizeable building.

In looking through my grandfather's letters I came across one in which he was applying for an increase in his police pension. One of the points he made in his letter was that he had just been reassessed in the Parish of Thurlestone on 'Woodbine' and the amount he had to pay had been raised from £6 to ten guineas per year. This was March, 1924. He went on to say: 'The house that I occupy is very old, formerly a barn turned into a dwelling house. It cost me over £100 last year in repairs.'

Suppose he was right, and 'Woodbine' had been a barn – then where was the farmhouse? Could it have been directly in front of 'Woodbine', right on the main road? It would explain the reason for the other cottage in 'Woodbine's' grounds – the place where my grandfather kept his cider barrels and which is now Brigadier Simon Gavourin's garage. Could that have been another of the farm buildings?

All this is, of course, mere speculation and I will never be able to prove it. All it shows is the way that the ownership of a cottage catches your imagination – and the way that imagination can run riot when you try to date an old building!

It was at this moment – just when I was letting imagination take over from fact, and just when I thought I would get no further for some time in dating the cottage – that I got the most stupendous clue of all.

I don't know about you, but if I find a book about an area or subject that interests me, then that book is a 'must' on my shopping list. I wouldn't go so far as to call this an insatiable quest for knowledge – it is really a desire not to miss anything interesting. But the book must be about something in which I am interested before I see it. For example, as I rarely catch an interest from a book, *Rat-Catchers of the 18th Century in Wiltshire* would interest me not at all, nor am I likely to want to know more about rat-catching in Wiltshire. But *Devon Life in 1580* would be essential reading – you see, I might find out something about Devon village life from it. And I am already interested in that.

It was this business of being able to find out something from a book, which made *Enjoying Archives* by David Iredale (David and Charles) catch my eye.

It is a good title and in my cottage-dating mood it captured my interest immediately. So I read it, and on page 123 I found this: 'Finally in 1836, the Tithe Commutation Act allowed the commutation (compulsory if necessary) of tithes into money payments.

'A village meeting agreed on the value of tithes based on average corn prices for the past seven years. Commissioners then awarded a rent-charge to be shared among all proprietors of property. A land surveyor drew up a very large-scale and coloured plan of the village or town, detailing every parcel of land, every path, garden, shed, outhouse, stream and factory. . . .'

And then came the vital words: 'Three copies are produced which today should be in the parish chest; diocesan registry or county record office; *and the Public Record Office'*

Mr Iredale was talking about my old friend, the Tithe Map of 1840 – the one which was undecipherable at the Devon Record Office in Exeter. What Mr Iredale was saying was that there should be another copy of the map in the Public Record Office in London.

The trouble with reading a book at the weekend is that you have to wait until Monday to follow up the clues. But bright and early I was on to the Public Record Office – I have held a Reader's ticket for years for research for my books on wrecks around the coasts of Britain – and met with the usual incredible (in this day and age!) help and advice.

Yes, they held copies of all the Tithe Maps. Thurlestone? How do you spell that? And my heart sank again into gloom when they said they had no map of that spelling. Could it be Thurleston? In Devon, yes. Now I remembered the changed spelling of the village over the years. Yes, that was probably it.

But I wasn't sure until I was in the Public Record Office in Chancery Lane a week later – it takes four days to get the maps up from whichever vault they are kept in – and unrolling a hand-drawn map of a very familiar area. Yes, it was the Tithe Map of Thurlestone, 'surveyed by John Tho. Tucker, Bridgetown, 1840' and with it went the Tithe Apportionment Book.

But if you expect to see a book as we know it today listing the apportionment of tithes you would be disappointed, for the 'book' is a roll of parchment-like papers. Compared with the two-foot deep 'book', the map is huge, taking in Bantham, Buckland and other villages.

Eagerly I looked for Thurlestone and having found it and identified the cottage, turned even more eagerly to the Tithe Apportionments.

The 'book' starts very grandly with George Louis 'duly appointed and sworn' as Assistant Tithe Commissioner for the 'Parish of Thurleston in the County of Devon'. He stated that he had called a meeting of the village to tell them of the Act and to find out details of their holdings.

Thurlestone Hotel before 1927. The steps on the left were originally for carrying corn up to the granary – the building's original use

The scene today. The building is now the inn and the luxury modern hotel is behind it

'Just-a-Cottage' as it is today

What happens when cob gives way! This is 'Woodbine's' front in 1944 when my mother owned it. 'Woodbine' has now, of course, been restored to its full beauty

He found 'that the lands of the said Parish are covered from the render of certain Tithes in kind by certain customary or prescriptive payments as follows:

'For every Cow one penny.

'For every Hogshead of Cider fourpence.

'For every Garden one penny.

'For every Hearth one penny.'

And George Louis went on to detail how he was going to change all that payment in kind into payment in money. Out of the 1,727 acres of the parish, he found that only 171 acres, two roods and eleven perches are the 'Sites of Houses, Courtlages, Hedges, Wastes, Sands, Beach, and Roads'.

He awarded £328 and ten shillings to be paid to the Rector under the new Act instead of all the original Tithes in kind. I bet the Rector was delighted. He must have had a great deal of difficulty persuading the Devon cottager that he should pay 'a penny a garden' or even 'a penny a hearth'. You can imagine them saying: 'But I never use it, Rector' . . . 'What hearth? – that's my sister's, Sir'.

I saw, too, in the book that seventy-three acres, one rood and thirty-three-and-a-half perches were not subject to tithes. And roads took up a further twenty-six acres, two roods and thirty-eight perches.

The speed with which I turned the crackling pages must have disturbed other researchers in the North Room of the Record Office. But I was desperately anxious to find out the details about my cottage. I must confess here that I had been disappointed in the map. An amateur could almost have done better. The houses and cottages, unless they had been moved in a landslide since 1840, were not quite in the right place. Near enough, but not quite right by today's better mapping standards.

My cottage was numbered '50' and I searched through the reference numbers in desperation. I noted that Ball Park, the field which had so often in our youth led the way to the adventurous walk to Bantham, had even then been called just that. But I noted too, with some surprise, that the field into which the footpath led before dropping down the hill was called 'East North Down' and the field just before the stream itself was called 'Oat Addish'.

But there was no trace in the details of fields and farms of No 50. It was with horror that I finally came to a page that was headed 'Cottages etc not subject to Tithes' – and, would you believe it, there was the number '50' with its size, two perches, and no other details!

There were no other details of any of the buildings in the village either. Sizes of land occupied – and the size of gardens, or land belonging, but nothing else.

George Louis, Commissioner of Tithes, had been, in my view, totally negligent. No one who owned a dwelling in Thurlestone had to pay any tithe rent on it. Fields, yes, but dwellings, no. And by agreeing to that, George Louis, whom I suspect retired a rich man, wiped out, at a stroke, one of the best sources of information about Thurlestone's past that we are ever likely to have had. However, I suspect that my fury at losing all that dating evidence is doing George a disservice. He was probably right in taxing the landowners and not the cottagers.

Could I then learn nothing from the Tithe Map? It does not seem to have been completed and received by the Tithe Commissioners until May, 1842 – at least, that is the date of their stamp upon it.

I pored over it – and then realised that I was missing something obvious. The other cottage which shared the site was numbered '49'. And it was marked down as exactly the same size – two perches.* That must mean that in 1840 the building was divided into two. Two cottages in one building. Not three as it was in about 1924.

So my cottage had been equal in size to the one now occupied by Leonard Jeffery. And if the Groses had had no difficulty in putting his cottage back into one from two, then it meant that my cottage had once been much bigger. So, obviously the building had once been one, then divided into two and only much more recently into three. Well, it's fascinating to speculate. But there were other things the Tithe Map told me.

It told me that a great deal of the land – according to the map – directly behind 'Woodbine' had belonged to the cottage

*A rood is a fourth part of a statute acre. A perch is a measure of length of five-and-a-half yards; a square perch, which is probably the measure referred to on the Tithe Map, is thirty-and-a-quarter square yards.

marked '49' on the map. Did this mean that my guess was right and that '49' and '50' (my cottage and that of Leonard Jeffery) were the main building and that 'Woodbine' had indeed been a barn, as my grandfather had said, belonging to the main house on the village street?

I don't know. What I do know from studying the map is that '49' and '50' between them owned twenty-seven perches and '196', which is now 'Woodbine', had only twelve perches of land and that included the smaller building which is now a store. The conclusion might indeed be that the two cottages, which are now small and own less land than 'Woodbine', were at that time more important than their bigger neighbour of today.

Further study of the map shows that in 1840 three buildings occupied the site now taken up by my next door neighbour with Home Cottage. It shows, too, that the village grew up the hill from the church, not down towards the sea. Maybe the seashore – and the land just behind it – were not safe places to build on in the troubled times when Thurlestone began to develop as a community. Certainly in 1840 there were no village buildings below the church on the road to the sea.

Peter Grose, owner of the superb modern Thurlestone Hotel, put his finger firmly on this point when he told me that he thought one had to look for the basic reason for the village's existence. Why should there be a village there at all? He felt it must have grown around a farm.

Further study of the map and its linked documents might well lead to other conclusions, but there for the moment, disappointed not to have found more definite information, I had to leave it.

For the moment, certainly, I had come to a full stop. I had spread a net of letters, but nothing more was coming in. So I got on with the chapters of this book which were within my own personal experience.

6. *Thatch and All That*

If I wanted to avoid the attentions of a traffic warden, create traffic chaos and still not get moved on by a policeman, I would be a thatcher. At least, I would be a West Country thatcher – I'm not so sure that it would work in Piccadilly!

For the truth is that thatching needs a bit of space. At some time or another the front of every Devon cottage needs re-thatching. And as most Devon thatched cottages front on to a road, thatching tends to bring most normal traffic movement to a slow crawl, if not a halt.

In Devon nobody minds. It is a job that needs to be done and when it is, out go the traffic cones and cars and lorries take it all in good part. Deep in the heart of every Englishman, and every tourist, is some sort of admiration for a craft. And thatching is a craft. Each time some roof needs re-thatching, the thatcher gathers his own little crowd, who watch and try to learn what it's all about.

As the owner of the property being thatched you have more right to know what is going on than anyone else. This right enables you to step inside the magic circle of straw or reed in the road and find out what goes on at first hand.

You will gather, I hope, that I speak from experience. The back of 'Just-a-Cottage' was done when the bathroom and other renovations took place, but the time came when the patching at the front could no longer stand up to the onslaught of rain.

To be fair, the thatcher who patched the front did it with little enthusiasm. He was then of the opinion that the whole front needed doing – and he was right. The only problem was that I did not have the money. The patching, as I remember it, cost about £20 and the cost of re-thatching, if it was to be the same as the cost of the back, would have worked out at something in the region of £144. The patching held for nearly two years – a fair amount of grace – and then it gave way with a rush.

It looked appalling – great dips between the ties, which I now know one should call 'spars' – and it seemed to get worse daily. Plants – presumably from bird-carried seeds – began to grow up there. But worse than that, water began sending its rust-red streaks down the bedroom ceilings and walls. It is interesting that the water-runs should be rust-coloured. There was no iron there to give it this tint, but I gather that the decomposition of wheat straw does over the years produce this hue.

Emergency action became necessary when water began pouring through into the bedroom in quantity. I must say, people are nice. The holidaymaker who had rented the cottage during the torrential downpour that had finally broken the thatch's back, merely moved the beds away from the inpour and asked mildly if something could be done. The patching had not lasted as long as I had hoped. But it was quite obvious that the thatch's time had come.

Now, you will read horrendous things about thatched cottages. You will be told that (a) no thatcher can be found at less than eight months' notice; (b) the cost of insuring a thatched cottage is more than man can pay; and (c) thatching is a dying craft and so the few survivors hold you up to ransom for all the money you have before they will lift a ladder to help you. All of which is nonsense.

Take (a) for example. Gordon Jeffery who, as I have already said, is the village builder and local handyman, found a thatcher for me in exactly one week flat – even if it did take the thatcher four weeks to find a day or two clear to start work on my cottage.

Take (b). The cost of insuring my cottage with the mortgage company is exactly £3.75 per year.

Take (c). The dying craft of thatching is far from dying; in fact, it is the healthiest growth cottage industry in the world. They have more work than they can handle and so recruits are coming forward all the time. Far from taking all the money you have before lifting a ladder to help you, there is an average payment. I was told recently that this works out in most parts of Devon at £75 per ten foot by ten foot square. They could hold you to ransom by reason of their over-stuffed order-books, but you will find it difficult to get a thatcher by paying over the odds. He has his future to think about and is much more interested in a long line of roofs behind him sheltering satisfied owners. Because most non-thatched owners do not realise that a newly-thatched roof is not a guarantee of no trouble for the next twenty or thirty years. If it were, there would be a lot of out-of-work thatchers around.

It is true that the main bulk of the roof will last for twenty, even forty, years. But the ridge of the roof will not last that long. The ridge needs attention every five or seven years – so each new roof the thatcher does means that his craft will be needed again in several years time to fix the ridge. 'You've got to care for thatch,' said my thatcher, almost as though we were talking about shampoo-ing hair!

Thatchers, among thatched-roof owners, evoke fierce loyalty. I must say, I found it amusing to be told that so-and-so was no use – 'Just look at the dip in that roof!' But was not so amused when my thatcher was even slightly criticised. But, of course, he did do a magnificent job and all such criticism was finally proved groundless!

Prices are going up – isn't everything? – but I found it upsetting to read that in November, 1971, a newspaper article about thatching which rated the cost of a square (the old ten by ten again) at £30 to £40 for wheat reed in Devon and £35 to £48 for Norfolk reed. I read, too, that at that time numbers of young entrants were queuing to get into the trade in the thatch country which lies below a line drawn between the Wash and Central Wales. Even so I was confident that my thatcher in 1973 would be one of those old craftsmen, bent and bowed by the demands of years and years on the thatch.

I had spoken to him on the telephone and his voice seemed an authentic part of old Devonshire. Yes, I wanted him to do it as soon as he could. Yes, he could start work whenever he liked. But there was a delay. I went down to the cottage expecting to see a new lemon-coloured roof, a roof which from my own personal observation takes nearly two years to change suddenly to the standard pale grey thatched roof colour. But there was the same old roof, fallen in even more than usual.

Where was my thatcher? Well, there had been problems. He had had 'flu – and no one in their right mind would expect a man with 'flu to work on a dusty roof. I despaired. But I needn't have done. During the course of a short stay at the cottage, my thatcher arrived. First of all I was a bit shaken that instead of some ancient hay cart, a van pulled up outside. True, it was an A30 which had seen better days, but it wasn't quite the image I had expected.

Nor was the thatcher who got out of it! David Trant was, I guess, in his late twenties, had long blonde hair and wore dark sun-glasses. I worried. But I needn't have done. From the van emerged cones to move the traffic away from the theatre of operations, a mountain of wooden pegs, that I was quickly told were called 'spars', ladders that looked old and very professional, and plenty of rope.

He had hoped, he told me, to have an even younger assistant, but the youngster had done himself an injury during Judo classes that stopped all ladder-climbing for a while. But he was going to carry on himself – even if it made the work a bit slower.

I think he sensed my anxiety for he told me of his apprenticeship to a man who was obviously locally renowned as a thatcher. He had come from Bovey Tracey and proposed to drive from there – over thirty miles – each day to attend to my roof. He felt he could do the whole front in three or four days. I felt that this seemed a short stay for a bill of £155.

I was wrong to doubt. Wrong to doubt David Trant, who made a fine job of the cottage roof. Wrong too, of course, to have doubted that Gordon Jeffery would supply me with anyone who would not give of their best.

The next few days passed with 'Just-a-Cottage' the centre of attraction in the village. I knew, because they told me, that many people were watching this young man to see what sort of job he made of my roof, so that they could then leap in and get him to work on their thatch.

David Trant was a man who planned ahead. The wheat reed was already stored at the side of Gordon Jeffery's house and the work went ahead apace. I was puzzled at first that his only demand on our facilities was for water. But then I learned. You see, explained David Trant, Norfolk reed grows in water and does not usually need watering. The wheat reed that now decorates 'Just-a-Cottage's' roof needs wetting before thatching.

I began to get one or two thatching terms straight. The pegs which hold the thatch down to the roof are, as I said earlier, called spars. You need to water wheat reed, which you and I would call straw, so that it bends, not breaks, as it is fitted and bent into the roof.

Would I not have been better off with Norfolk reed, that substance which is mentioned with bated breath by those who know no better? Answer, yes – if I wanted to start from scratch. It would be no good putting Norfolk reed on top of a wheat straw base. The only result would be that the reed would bend when the spars were put in, but would unbend as time passed and so pull off all the thatch. The end product of this mixing would be a cottage without a roof and the lot on the ground around! So Norfolk reed needs nailing with special iron grips to the rafters.

To the onlooker, the preparation seems the major part of thatching – and I don't suppose that anyone would argue about the truth of this. David Trant would select his straw with care, tap it carefully against the road surface until all the stems were in perfect line and then with expert twists tie each 'parcel' with a 'rope' of the same straw.

His hands bore the marks of recent blisters and though I supposed these were the result of actual thatching, they were not. The blisters he had got after agreeing with a farmer friend that he would buy all the straw from the farmer's wheat crop. (A thatcher must lay in a stock of straw, just as a builder must have a supply of bricks.) Part of the deal was that David Trant must supply the labour to bind and stook his own reed. It was a mammoth task resulting in 800 sheafs for the roofs of Devon. It seemed an awful lot of work – surely he could buy the straw after the combine harvester had passed? Trant twitched almost as though I had sworn at him. Combine harvester's leavings are, it seems, not good enough for a thatcher's needs.

All this information, you must realise, was gleaned between his trips up and down the ladder to the roof of my cottage. In between pieces of information, I watched him walk the thatch, tearing out the old and putting a good two or three feet of new thatch in its place. The ends of each 'sheaf' were smacked into place with an instrument that looked for all the world like the 'bats' that used to be used on an aircraft carrier to indicate to the incoming pilot whether he was high or low. It is called a 'leggett' in this area. The ends over the windows were cut with a huge pair of shears into a smooth U-curve.

Watching him and squinting up at the sun, I admired the way he walked on the thatch. Do thatchers never fall? For an answer he showed me a repaired ladder. As he had stood on the end the cross-bar of the first step had given way – and so had all the others as the ladder splayed out into the equivalent of a huge pair of stilts. That had been bad enough, but the snapping had disturbed all his fastenings – including the ropes, which on my cottage lashed the end of the main ladder tight in to the hooks of the old gateway to 'Woodbine'.

So, trapped in the wreckage of his broken ladder he had plunged down the roof and landed on his back in the road. He lay there, gingerly testing each limb and only when he was convinced all were intact did a stream of oaths, not peculiar to Devonians, spray into the air.

For a comparatively young man he was already full of stories about his trade. He didn't fancy wire-meshing over the thatch and had a theory that not only did it not keep out the birds, but if a 'slide' started in any place the wire would hold the whole thing together and pull off the entire roof.

He made my wife, Penny, pull a wry face when he described the things he finds in the thatch – birds are just commonplace, but dead cats were not unusual and so was something else that he strongly suspected of being too large for a cat, more like a dog!

Slowly, as the thatching went on, the mound of discarded straw, or reed, call it what you will, grew around the front of the cottage. First the front door disappeared and then the downstairs windows. And soon we had the lights on as straw mounted right up and over the upstairs windows. It is amazing how much comes off – and even how much is left. I gather from David Trant that our thatch, thick as it was, was a mere nothing compared with one of his earlier jobs.

It seems that a thirteenth century manor house needed thatching in his territory, and the architect involved in other matters needed at the same time to find the ridge pole of the roof. Young Trant was selected to find the ridge. In the end he dug down seven feet through the old thatch – and when he was standing on the ridge could only indicate his position by waving a hand from the top of his vertical tunnel.

Having seen how much thatch came off my own modest structure, I can believe completely David Trant's report that by the time they had finished taking off the old thatch the drive to the manor house led, not to a house, but to derelict hay-rick, for the house had disappeared completely. He says it took them three weeks to cart the old thatch away.

We had to leave before the final touches were put to the roof and one of our holiday tenants moved in. Having seen how much straw was all about and how it penetrated into the house, I had no hesitation in granting the tenant a discount when he complained, nicely, of the inconvenience the thatching had caused him. On the other hand, there are not many holidays from which you can return and say, casually 'They re-thatched us while we were on holiday this year. . . .' But then such a statement might be misinterpreted!

All in all, we wouldn't be without our thatch. One thing you cannot argue about; a thatched cottage is not only a pretty cottage – it's a snug one. The way the thatch holds the warmth in winter, and the cool in summer is worth a lot of trouble every twenty years!

7. Knobs and Knockers

When you start furnishing an old cottage, you may start off with very fixed ideas about the way you want it to look, but I will guarantee that once started you will never stop.

You see, the trouble, or rather the pleasure, of it all is that even if you make up your mind that your cottage is going to be predominantly, say, Victorian, then other items of furniture will turn up which don't fit in with your plans, but you will not be able to discard them.

I've told you about my grandfather's travelling trunk, and the hat-boxes which we turned into waste-paper baskets. So in a way we had set the theme of the cottage. It was going to be Victorian, because most of the furniture we set out with dates from that period. I can't say that we turned to each other and said, 'Let's make it a Victorian cottage', because we didn't. But you'll find that you are lured away from being too rigid about the decorations by the simple fact that a cottage has to be comfortable as well as period.

Now I am sure that pedants will disagree with me, but I am very willing to go on record by saying that comfort was one thing that the Victorians were not very good at, even in their calmer moments. So you've got to strike a balance.

I don't think we have got it right at the cottage yet – for the simple reason we have to think of the comfort of our guests. And their comfort does depend to a certain extent on not laying traps for them and their children.

It is no good, for example, putting a splendid example of a Victorian oil lamp somewhere where children can pull it down and break it. In fact, it would be totally unfair to do so.

So you'll find if you have a cottage and intend to let it, that your own home gets cluttered with things that you intend for the cottage when you've finished with the letting game. The temptation is to take such things down to the cottage and lock them away. But if your cottage is as small as ours you'll find that this restricts the amount of space available to guests for storage. So you can't do it.

Of course, it won't stop you from snapping up items at antique shops which you know will be perfect for the cottage in the fullness of time, but it is frustrating not to be able to put your treasures on display.

The possession of the cottage drives you – at least it does me – into wandering round antique shops with only your cottage in mind. In other words, the ownership of the cottage drives you into fields that you would never have explored otherwise. Before I had the cottage I wouldn't have looked in every antique shop window when I walked past. I do now.

I have learned, too, all sorts of things that I never even knew existed in my pre-cottage days. One of the most rewarding fields opened up when I noticed a new shop called 'The Welsh Dresser' on Gipsy Hill near my home in South London. To me then the now normal habit of stripping old furniture of its near-black vanish and bringing up the natural colours of the wood with ordinary furniture polish, was a revelation.

The table that we then had in the cottage was a very ordinary one, with brown-varnished legs and a kitchen top with drawers underneath on one side. I looked at the glowing cottage furniture in 'The Welsh Dresser' and in my mind saw it gleaming away in the cottage in Devon. 'The Welsh Dresser' is owned by Mrs Margaret Corlett, and she and her sister were not at all secretive about the way to restore old furniture to modern beauty. But they did warn me that certain furniture will never come up as well as other items. It all depends on the original wood.

Penny and I set to work on the kitchen table in 'Just-a-Cottage'. For your guidance the way to do it is this: You need a liquid stripper called 'Nitromors', an old washing-up brush, some wire-wool, plenty of wet cloths, and a liberal supply of warm water. And, most important of all, plenty of room to make a mess, somewhere out of doors where stains on the ground will not matter.

Pour some stripper on the article to be cleaned and agitate it with the washing-up brush all over a small section of the surface. As you do this you will see the stain of years start to come off in great gooey liquid waves. When you think that you are down to the bare wood, wash it away with a very wet cloth. It is best to use rubber gloves for this operation. You'll never be able to use them for anything again, but it does save you from having peculiarly-stained hands for some days afterwards. Be very careful to keep the stripper away from your face and eyes. If some does drip on to bare flesh you will feel it sting, but a liberal application of fresh water will stop any real damage. Repeat the application of the stripper until you have the kind of surface you want.

Old varnishes seem to have been made up from a most incredibly tacky solution and you will soon be surrounded by stained plastic bowls, impossibly dirty cloths and stains on the ground where the gunk has dripped from the article you are cleaning. We use the wire-wool very rarely and then only to break the surface of some odd carving or curly surface that will not give way to the stripper at once.

Though 'Nitromors' is incredibly efficient, don't expect miracles. It is hard work and often needs several applications to remove all the old varnish. Think before you start work. Look in today's antique shops and see if you think your old furniture will be improved by stripping. Some of the furniture on display would, I think, have been better left as it was. At least the layers of old varnish covered imperfections. But once the wood is laid bare they will stand out for all to see. And, of course, this is not the way to treat some very old piece that depends for some of its beauty on the glow from centuries of hand-polishing. In those cases nothing so crude as stripping should be used.

I said that it doesn't work with all furniture – and our kitchen table was one example where it made very little improvement. The table was a little lighter, but the basic wood was not very good and we were not pleased. This failure drove us into buying a new table for the cottage.

In 'The Welsh Dresser' they had some wonderful tables. Not old, but made from old beams from demolished houses in chunky country style, and then polished to a lovely mellow yellow by the liberal application of furniture polish. So we bought one – and a matching bench – and now it looks as though it was always part of the cottage. It wasn't cheap by any means, but in its position in front of the window seat, it seems to us well worth it.

Despite the failure of our experiment in stripping the original table, we had seen what stripping could do and now had several new ideas. The downstairs room, despite the newly-whitened walls, was dominated by my Uncle's great dresser. Almost jet-black, it seemed to darken the whole room. We knew its history – it had been a wedding present for my Uncle Charlie and Auntie Bea and had been specially made by a local craftsman.

We decided each time we saw it that it would be much improved by stripping, but each time we decided to do it we were beaten back by its very size and the shortage of time during our stays at the cottage.

The dresser performed a very useful function in the cottage. It contained, in its numerous drawers and cupboards, all the cutlery and crockery for the whole place. Unloading it seemed a major job in itself, but one day we finally got down to it, and dragged it into the yard at the back of the cottage for Operation Big Strip.

I know both Penny and I had our doubts about it before we started. I argued with myself that a local craftsman would be certain to have used good wood and, anyway, nothing could be worse than the standard Victorian black stain in which it was liberally daubed. At any rate, once we had lugged it outside we were committed.

At first the stain refused to budge but then the familiar gooey gloop started to roll down the untreated portions. One thing I should have warned you about stripping is that at first the stripped area looks very dull and unwanted, but it always looks better when the water you use to wash the stripper off has dried away. We had our doubts about that dresser. But slowly a nice mellow golden-brown wood emerged from beneath the stain and when we had finished we had high hopes of what a decent polish would do.

There are two ways of dealing with the stripped furniture after all the mess of stripping is over. One is to coat it liberally with furniture polish and then use elbow-grease. The other – more suitable in our case when most of the time we are not there to polish – is to use a coat of International Yacht Paint clear varnish. I think that the furniture polish method ends up best, but you have got to keep at it. We were very satisfied with the dresser after a coat of clear varnish.

We had, of course, removed all the drawer handles before stripping. These had been gun-metal pull-handles and though they were undoubtedly the best thing in their day, Penny and I decided that brass handles would set the whole thing off so much better. Which thought – in a cottage one thing always does lead you to another – led us to the world of brass-handles, knobs and knockers. Which in turn led us to . . . but that will come in due course.

I would have thought it impossible to match the pull-handles from the dresser, but it was obvious that the antique shops, which all now seemed to specialise in stripped furniture, were getting new brass fittings from somewhere.

A few inquiries and our problems were solved. 'What you want to do,' said someone knowledgeably, 'is to go to Knobs and Knockers'. Well, it did sound the sort of place we needed – and we found it in Judd Street, W.C.1.

Now, 'Knobs and Knockers' is the cottage fanatic's dream of a shop come true. Hanging there on display boards were not only every kind of brass fitting you could want, in most cases copies of antique originals, but also everything the cottage improver could desire.

There were door-knobs of all shapes and sizes, door finger panels (we bought some particularly pretty ones with flowers set under glass for the bedroom doors), door knockers, many superb copies of antique originals, letter box frames, keyhole covers, cast-iron work, brass lamps, whole doors, bathroom ware. . . . It was the most fantastic collection of cottagey goods I have ever seen. So we dived in and bought our pull-handles, identical with the gun-metal originals but in polished brass, and some handles of the swivel-drop kind for the old chests I was stripping and refurbishing. The temptation is to buy everything that might prove useful at some future date, for you do get a lot of ideas from the displays. Fortunately, before we completely overspent, we had to leave to collect one of the children from school.

'Knobs and Knockers' have branches in Manchester, Leeds, and Kingston in Surrey, but if you are really in the wilds they have a good mail-order service. Their goods are not cheap, but what delight is? Each of our drawer pulls cost 25p, but I should warn you that one of the dangers of such a shop is that, after a visit, you may tend to strip a painted wooden chest just for the pleasure of putting brass corners on it and brass handles at each end!

The change in a man or woman who buys an old country cottage is amazing to behold. Now we have them delving into old records to date it. Visiting antique shops to furnish it. Stripping furniture for the pleasure of it. Buying brass handles to embellish it. And as the cottage has changed our life, we speak from experience!

But not all the strange things that cottage people do are listed above. I have missed out several changes that will come over normally sane people, but one of the worst diseases, as my wife, Penny, will tell you is the one called the 'Old Lamp Fever'. Beware! It is terribly catching.

When we first looked over the contents of the cottage after we bought it, I had not got the disease. I know I hadn't, because I gave my sister, Christine, a brass oil lamp that was there for her home. Now I have the disease, whenever I go down to Dorset I look at that lamp and wonder how I ever came to give her such a fine specimen. And though I am not potty about silver-handled Victorian umbrellas, I should perhaps warn my younger sister, Mavis, that the one I gave her from the cottage might be snatched back at any moment if I catch the 'Old Umbrella Infection'!

Lamps are particularly contagious. Lampmen or lamp-women are liable to describe how they found such-and-such a specimen in some remote place, how they paid only pence for it, and how they saw the same thing priced at £40 in some chic antique shop in Town.

Victorian oil lamps are becoming more and more difficult to find at reasonable prices. One that I bought in a Cornish village for £7 had its identical twin on sale recently at a local 'antiques fair' for £34. It is commonplace now to see really ugly specimens that sold in Harrods in the 1890's for a few shillings – old catalogues make such fascinating reading that publishers are bringing them out in hardcovers – on sale for £20 or £30.

Dealers have cleaned out whole areas. One told me that he

had worked for six weeks in one area of North Wales to find local specimens and, though he was selling them in the suburbs of London for £10 a time, he had paid practically nothing for them in Wales. Such times are, my antique dealer acquaintances assure me, now over. People have much more idea about the value of their grandparents possessions and tend to get a proper valuation of items before handing them over to their friendly neighbourhood junk man.

Yet it is still possible to pick up a good brass oil lamp for a pound or two. It won't have the glass of course, but that is easily remedied. I bought one during the writing of this book for £2 – but perhaps that was only because I was buying an old Victorian wash-bowl and jug stand for three times as much.

With oil lamps you are competing, not only with enthusiasts in this country, but also with the vast American market. Incidentally, those Victorian bathroom sets – bowl, jug, soap dish and smaller jug – often beautifully decorated with roses and other colourful scenes, are mostly on their way to the United States too. I am told that whole shiploads go across the Atlantic for which dealers in this country have paid only £2 per set – and which fetch fantastic prices in the States. My advice would be to hang on to any original jugs and bowls you possess – at the rate they are disappearing, you'll not only have something attractive, but also worth a fortune when the supply in this country runs out, as it soon must.

But we are getting a long way away from oil lamps. I said earlier on that you would often find that the glass of the lamp you bought had not survived. This, just as brass handles drove us to 'Knobs and Knockers' will undoubtedly drive you to another London shop for a replacement. The shop rejoices under the name of 'Christopher Wray's Lighting Emporium' and you'll find it in the Kings Road, S.W.6.

Here is what I guess to be the largest collection of oil lamps under one roof in the Kingdom. It is a bewildering show – and a totally fascinating one. The entire ceiling and most of the walls and floors are festooned with lamps – oil and gas lamps, restored lamps, ships' lamps, wall lamps, hanging lamps, heater lamps – you name it, they've got it.

In addition to all that, the Emporium can supply lamp

chimneys to match your lamp base, shades of all kinds, burners, galleries, brass founts. By taking your base along there you can turn it back to its original condition. What I liked in particular was the knowledge of the assistants. One very pretty girl told me that I had the wrong chimney on one of mine – it should have been straight and tall, not one with a bulge in what I call the 'burning area'.

So, you see, I learnt as I went along. I restored and cleaned what I could. But I had, of course, some genuine things. For example, I hung my grandfather's police truncheons, decorated with 'VR' and gold crowns and the numbers '54' and '55', by the downstairs mirror and felt they added a touch of law and order to a cottage whose furnishings we have not yet got under control.

And talking of restoring things – the preservation order is still there on the front of the cottage, and for all I know has been dropped back on the rear now that I have put in a proper kitchen and bathroom. The gate to the 'tunnel' under our large bedroom which leads through to 'Woodbine', had suffered most from the passage of time. Though the basic frame of heavy ironwork had stood up to rough treatment – including my sisters and I swinging on it during our holidays in Thurlestone years ago (it used to drive Uncle Charlie and Auntie Bea wild if they caught us at it) – the vertical bars had resisted less strongly the attacks of rust.

As a result, the spade points of this piece of nineteenth century workmanship became positively dangerous. In fact, one visitor cut his hand on it. In view of the preservation order I felt that the gate ought to be replaced by one which was exactly the same as the original. The quote I got from wrought iron workers and blacksmiths in the London area – yes, there are a few if you search them out – appalled me. They ranged from £20.55(excluding VAT) right up to £50.50 (including VAT).

Local people I told of this were horrified, which is why the gate was lifted off its hinges and taken in to Norman Simcox at the Ebrington Forge in Kingsbridge. His price for repairing the gate and delivering it back to Thurlestone was exactly £10. Which only goes to show that you can't beat local work – or prices!

It was while studying the gate that I noticed two hooks let into the wall to one side of the front door of 'Just-a-Cottage'. I wondered why I hadn't noticed them before and then decided that I must have done, but in the rush of 'whitewashing' the outside of the cottage had had no time to stop and stare.

Looking at them now it was obvious that a door had been hung on them – not the gate to the passageway because they were in the wrong position for that. Studying old photographs of the village street made me think that at one time the door of the cottage had been of the stable kind, with the top opening independently of the bottom.

And then I remembered, went looking for, and found, the bottom half of a stable door that had turned up during our attack on the sheds in the garden. I tried it on the hooks. It almost fitted but not quite. It was also clear that a stable door was the only possible explanation of the hooks.

At that time – almost as though it had been planned – we started to have trouble with the front door to the cottage. It was clear that low down on the right hand side as you looked in from the street, a piece of the door frame had rotted. The door stuck. When it was wet, it swelled and was almost impossible to open. When it was dry, you could almost see the gap between the door and the wall.

So I asked Gordon Jeffery if he could make us an old-fashioned stable door. It was a silly question really. Of course he could. So we moved back to the original style of door of the cottage when he made and fitted – taking out the rotted part of the frame – a stable door. This solved the problem experienced by many cottage owners in similar circumstances. The cottage door literally opens on to the main street. In high summer you have a problem. You want more air in the cottage, but if you open an ordinary full-length door you open it, not only to dogs and cats, but also to the end of privacy.

If you look down the village you will see many stable doors on the cottages. It is the complete answer to the need for privacy and also for fresh air. And more important as far as 'Just-a-Cottage' is concerned, it is a return to the way it was in the past.

8. *Bodies on the Beach*

When you want to find out about something in South Devon, you have only to ask. It isn't like that in other parts of the country. Try asking, as I have during the course of my work as a journalist, a Durham miner the cause of trouble at the pit and you'll be lucky if he answers you at all. He may spit on your shoes, but he will tell you nothing of what you want to know!

But the Devon man, he'll tell you if you approach him the right way. I think it's all a matter of confidence. The Devon man will appreciate your interest, but, be warned, he is inclined to a bit of leg-pulling. He's no dimmy – and don't think he is! Which is why I was prepared for – and took – a fair amount of leg-pulling about things I wanted to know for the chapters in this book.

For example, when I was a child, the idea of bathing at Bantham was just not on. There were great notices, and they – or ones like them – are there to this day, which spell out in great capital letters that if you do bathe there at certain states of the tide then you may die.

We were told as children that the dreaded quicksands of Bantham would swallow you up if you so much as set foot on the beach. And as a result the idea of bathing there never entered our heads. We played on the sand dunes – a marvellous place for courting couples – all held together with reeds and grasses that thrived in such conditions. But bathe? No, never.

In fact, in Thurlestone Churchyard is a grim warning of the perils of doing so – and the epitaph 'drowned bathing at Bantham' dates back to the early 1850's. It was therefore terribly puzzling to go back to Bantham in recent times and find not only that the whole area was devoted to the sport of surfing, but that our fears of yesteryear were, apparently, groundless.

The sight of surfers, complete with black wet-suits, waiting for a wave was extraordinary. They stood in the very parts that we had been told as children was most dangerous. Why were not the dreaded quicksands gobbling them up willy-nilly?

The best place to find the answer to any local question is in the local. And Bantham is blessed with a marvellous, and extraordinary, local – the fifteenth century Sloop Inn.

Dennis Cresdee and his wife own the Sloop and they take a great interest in the history of the area. The Sloop is old, without any doubt. In the public bar the floor is uneven enough to be the original fifteenth century flagstones. It is here that you will find the surfers (and the members of the Surf Life Saving Club), sometimes still dripping in wet-suits as they drink their beer or cider. If their faces are red it is not entirely due to the fumes of their drinks, but more likely to the whip and sting of cold storm waves which they seek out, even in winter, for the thrill of the ride on their surf-boards.

Yet while surfers drink on one side of the bar, on the right of their haunt lies another. I called the Sloop extraordinary. And I was right, for on that other side of the bar lies not only a cosy saloon, complete with yet another dart-board and even a mini-organ for late sweet music, but, further round still, a sophisticated dining room that gives you the impression of dining in a ship's saloon. Here the Cresdee's serve *cordon bleu* meals to dry-suited diners who travel from miles around to eat in oil-lamp lit sophistication. To get in you usually have to book.

Dennis Cresdee has a somewhat similar dating problem over the Sloop that I have over my cottage. Not about the date of building the old inn for that is firmly set in the 1400's. No, Dennis Cresdee's problem is who turned a single storey building into two? In other words, who put the top on the Sloop, and when?

I couldn't help him with that, but he told me of storms in the area which every now and again washed human bones out of the local beaches. I was not surprised at this; later in this book you will see just how many ships came to grief along these local shores. The number of ships that died hereabouts may, on the other hand, not surprise you. But why were the drowned buried on the beaches? Because they were – that is where the bones come from.

In actual fact, when a major sea disaster happened in the

days before the beginning of the nineteenth century and the dead were washed ashore in hundreds – some descriptions, particularly of the beaches after the sinking of a troop transport, tell of rows and rows of bodies on one single beach – they were usually buried quickly in a mass grave near the spot.

And if the dead from such a wreck were treated this way, there was even smaller care taken of the unidentified bodies found on some beach in the morning light with nothing to tell who they were, where they came from or indeed what ship had sunk under them. Stripped of clothes and any valuables, the naked corpses were tossed into a nearby sandhill or hummock and a few shovelfulls of sand thrown over them.

It wasn't until July, 1808, that an Act of Parliament required bodies cast ashore to be buried in a churchyard's consecrated ground. Only then do headstones start to record the toll of unknown sailors, so imagine how great a multitude who died in the sea before then now lie in unmarked graves! Lie, that is, until some great storm sends the waves digging into their last resting place in the sand. . . .

Actually, the history of things being washed out of the sand at Bantham goes back a long, long way. The dunes themselves – on the left-hand side of the mouth of the River Avon – are known as Bantham Ham. 'Ham' was the Saxon word for dwelling place (hence 'hamlet') and Bantham Ham certainly seems to have been that. The great storm of November 27th, 1703, which destroyed Eddystone Lighthouse*, and killed over 8,000 men in ships around Britain, did not spare South Devon. In fact, Bantham Ham was ripped and washed clear by huge waves driven on by the hurricane which devastated the rest of Britain.

And out from the Bantham Ham came clear evidence of the fact that this had been a dwelling place in the years long ago. Roman pottery was exposed, so was a stone axe, split bones, and the antlers of a red deer. The Ham, too, seems to have been the landing place of some Irish pirates in 1067. The Exeter version of the Domesday Book records this. Though the area referred to could just possibly be Thurlestone Sands, Bantham seems to have been their base of operations.

Wherever they were based, the Irish marauders seem to

*See *The Wreck Detectives* (George G. Harrap & Co Ltd)

have been mightily successful. They laid waste not only the manor of Thurlestone, but also those of Huish, Galmpton, Bagdon, Alston, Ilton, Collaton, Sewer (probably Soar) and Portlemouth. And then had the cheek to re-embark on to their ships at Salcombe and apparently get clean away with it!

The idea of the calm of the coast from Bantham to Salcombe being put to the sword does, I think, make you look differently at that wonderful cliff walk from Thurlestone to Hope and Hope to Salcombe. You are walking in peace along a path which others trod, swords at the ready, in search of blood, loot and rape.

And it isn't as though others who passed this way so many years ago have not left their mark. The Anglo-Saxons who colonised the West Country have left traces of their passing everywhere – in the South Devon names of places.

Combe at the end of a name is from 'cumb' meaning a narrow valley. Ham, as in Bantham Ham, means dwelling place. The ending to a name of 'ton' means farm, village or homestead. 'Worthy' means the same. 'Leigh' as an ending means a woodland glade; 'stow', a holy place and 'stoke', a church or monastery; 'more', a lake; 'well', a spring, often with a religious significance. 'Ford' is obvious. 'Borough', as in Malborough, meant a fortified place and that could include a manor, even a town.

But the words that will mean most to all who travel and admire the South Hams – the 'dwelling places in the South' – are the names for all the great headlands which dominate the scene.

'Bolt' means an arrow – hence Bolt Head and Bolt Tail. 'Prawle' comes from the Saxon word for winking and so indicates a place from which to watch – a look-out place. Start, another great promontory, comes from the word 'steort' meaning a tail – and what a mighty tail of the land Start Point is!

But I have wandered far from Bantham and the dreaded quicksands. The truth is that there are no quicksands. But Dennis Cresdee sent me to the expert – and he lived in Thurlestone, right on my own doorstep. Or if not quite as close as that, certainly in the village.

The man who knows most about the dangers of swimming in the area is, without doubt, Derrick Yeoman of Parkfield,

Thurlestone. Not only has he been Chairman of the Bantham Surf Life Saving Club since 1960, but he is also Beach Safety Officer for the Kingsbridge Rural District Council – a job which covers not only Bantham but all the beaches in the area.

He put my mind at rest almost as soon as we met about the quicksands at Bantham. He agrees with me that they do not exist. What the Victorians regarded as quicksands are in actual fact rip currents which sweep across the beach at certain states of tide, wind and weather. The current runs from right to left as you stand on the Hams and look out to sea. It is strong, too strong to fight even for a champion swimmer.

If caught in this cross-current, you will be swept along from right to left and then when approaching the rocks on the left-hand side of the bay, you will find you are fed out to sea. In these circumstances you must remain calm. I know it is easy to say, but local experts will by now – having seen what is happening – be making arrangements for your rescue.

I think the best thing I can do here, in the interests of local bathing safety, is to reproduce part of the contents of a leaflet which was produced by Mr Maitland Tribe for bathers in the area:

‘THE BATHERS’ GUIDE TO THE SOUTH HAMS OF DEVON

There are some twenty-five bathing beaches between the Dart and the Erme; every one of them is safe under normal conditions for bathers who use common sense and learn what local hazards to avoid.

The flat sandy beaches of Challaborough, Bigbury and Bantham offer the best opportunities for surfing, while the steep beaches of Start Bay are better for swimmers who like to get straight into deep water. At Blackpool, Slapton Sands, Beesands and Hallsands there are long stretches of beach unencumbered by rocks and seaweed.

Except near Start Point, where currents are very strong, there is little danger from currents, which tend to run parallel to the beach rather than out to sea, but during and after winds from the south and east there may be a heavy swell with a strong undertow which is dangerous to bathers. There are a number of small, flatter beaches between Start Point and Salcombe; these are safe except in rough seas; the best for surfing is Gara Rock, where the only hazards are outgoing tidal currents on the left of the beach for two hours each side of high water and on the right for two hours each side of low water.

There are safe sandy beaches, ideal for children, inside the bar at Salcombe, where dangerous surf is rare. Care is needed, however, to avoid the strong tidal current which sweeps up and down the middle of the Harbour, being at its strongest at half tide. North of the Ferry, on the East Portlemouth side, there are apt to be pits in the sand which can be dangerous to non-swimmers.

Between Bolt Head and Bolt Tail is Soar Mill Cove with a fine expanse of sand at low tide. The temptation to swim to the Ham Stone should be resisted owing to the strong tide which sweeps along this coast, particularly at high water and low water. Inner Hope Cove has a flat sandy beach, sheltered except from the West and it sometimes offers good surfing possibilities. The Thurlestone beaches are free from strong currents but are liable to dangerous undertow in heavy surf.

Bantham is the best surfing beach in the district, but it is definitely dangerous for those who ignore local advice. Heavy surf, as elsewhere, has its hazards, but the chief danger is the strong current which runs from right to left and then turns out to sea when it reaches the rocks on your left (as you face the sea). This may occur at almost any state of the tide and is accentuated by north-west winds. Bathers should at all times keep well to the right of the line of red and yellow buoys.

The beach is patrolled at week-ends by the Bantham Surf Life Saving Club which operates a fast rescue boat, and the Kingsbridge R.D.C. maintain a Hicks reel and line and a klaxon alarm. In emergency, a red flag may be hoisted and a rocket fired as a S.O.S. to nearby boats. About half-way down the beach there is often a channel stretching right across the main beach. Soon after high water the tide runs strongly out of this from right to left, but at low water it makes an excellent safe shallow bathing pool for small children.

When the tide comes in again, however, over the sand bank on the seaward side, people bathing in the open sea from this bank are cut off from the shore by a rapidly deepening channel. This can be avoided if they keep well to their left as they come ashore. During the week the beach is patrolled by a professional Life Guard employed by Kingsbridge R.D.C.

At Bigbury the safest beach is the north-west or right-hand side of the sand bar leading to the Island. On the south-facing beaches and at Sedgwell Cove the ebb tide runs out of the river very strongly and on the flood tide swimmers too far out may get carried across to Bantham and out to sea. Anyone intending to wade or swim to the Island should note that the water is deepest close to the Island and on a falling tide there is an outgoing current close to the rocks on your right as you approach the Island slipway. When the tide is running in strongly over the bar, particularly with a north-west wind, there is a current running towards the river.

At Sedgwell Cove bathers should beware of pits which sometimes form in the sand there. A Hicks reel and line and a klaxon are stationed here and the Bigbury Surf Life Saving Club covers the beach at week-ends, supported during the week by a lifeguard employed by the Council. A reef of rocks on the left of the Island, as you look from the mainland, is flanked on the side nearest Bigbury, by a deep, steeply shelving pool which, even at low tide, is a danger to non-swimmers and is subject to strong currents on a falling tide. The danger area is indicated by a red cross on the rock.

Challaborough has a flattish beach which is generally safe, except when there is a heavy swell and a red flag is flown. Bathers should avoid a seaward current at low water spring tides on the right of the beach facing the sea where there is a deep pool. There may also be current close to the rocks on the left and a bank and channel across the mouth of the cove. At Challaborough there is a Hicks reel, klaxon and tide clocks.

If you indulge in what is known as a 'midnight bathe' – an unwise hazard and not recommended – do not go alone; keep together and frequently check the number of your party, as in darkness one member can easily be lost.'

9. *The Salcombe Saga*

If you plan to spend much time in the South Hams of Devon and you have a large car, you will soon realise that it is not suitable for the winding lanes. In the best of all possible worlds, of course, you would have one fast monster for the run down on some motorway and then another, possibly a Mini, for sight-seeing and working trips about the area.

In a big car you spend a great deal of travelling time backing into those passing places cut out of the red soil and luxuriant hedge-growth to let the normal work-a-day vehicles – lorries, vans and green buses – go by. Try using a big car and pulling a boat on its own trailer behind you – and you will know what frustration means. It is, however, a tribute to the calm that comes over visitors to this high-banked land of narrow lanes to say that temper rarely shows. It is more likely that both vehicles in a confrontation will back away to find a passing place and then realise what has happened only when both are snugly tucked into the hedge and fifty yards apart.

Laughter is more likely to be the result of such a deferred meeting than any other reaction. I, truly, find this extraordinary. The same man who, in London Town, would fight you every wing-ripping inch of the way to some gap in the rush-hour traffic, will, even after a nerve-fraying drive down to Devon, smile and give way with perfect grace once he is confined in some leafy passage to a South Devon beach.

I mention this because we found that the perfect escape from the confines of a tiny cottage—especially decorating it!—is to take to estuary or river in a boat. The boat we already have, because of my passion for diving to explore the underwater wonderland that lies off any beach in the country. And when you see how clear the water is off the South Devon coast, you will understand that this is more than wonderland underwater – it is the anwer to a diver's prayer. But even if you don't wish to explore underwater, a boat is still the passport to another world in the Thurlestone, Bantham, Salcombe area.

The boat we have is one of the big C-craft inflatables – thirteen feet six inches long, beamy, and powered by a forty-five hp Chrysler outboard. Flat out it will do nearly thirty knots – and that on water is really travelling!

But the world into which I want to introduce you is not one of high-speed snarling engines. Save that for the open sea. In the world of Salcombe Estuary, Avon up to Aveton Gifford, or even Yealm at Newton Ferrers, high speed is not allowed. It is frowned upon, and quite right too.

It is odd, that in this world where towing a boat through narrow roads can become a lengthy procedure, the facilities for launching such a boat are superb. You have, of course, to pay a great deal of attention to the tides, but apart from that the actual meeting of boat keel to water is child's play.

Approaching Salcombe from Kingsbridge or Thurlestone, turn left at signs for 'Boat park' and you will find the best facilities I know. Down by the creek there is not only a car park, but if you push on, bearing left, you will find a well-organised trailer park and a proper concrete launching ramp which will take all manner of boats, even big ones, up to one hour from low water.

You can, of course, use the launching site in the centre of town, but I don't fancy your chances in the height of the reason when this popular car park is very full. You have to pay harbour dues wherever you launch and will have to display a sticker on your boat to show you have as well as one on your outboard engine. There is also an eight mile an hour speed limit in the estuary itself.

But this is the joy of Salcombe estuary. No one is really in a hurry. Parked out among the thousands of boats on buoys, you'll find the Salcombe Lifeboat. She is the only one to whom the speed-limit does not apply! And there could be a time when you'll be glad of that!

We have launched so often at this ramp at Batson Lake which is just one arm of the estuary, that I hesitate to point out that though nowadays it is known as Shadycombe, the Admiralty chart of the area calls it 'Shabbicombe'. Be that as it may, take the Admiralty Chart with you (it is listed as Chart No 28 'Salcombe Harbour') for this is your guide to marvellous creeks and views.

On a fine day you can chug up to Kingsbridge. You could launch there from the car park at the foot of the town, but only within two-and-a-half hours of High Water. (Pay attention to your return unless you fancy wading in deep mud!) Once at Kingsbridge, you can tie up to the wall of the Crabshell Inn and eat baskets of scampi or other sustaining food.

In fact, one of my most happy memories is motoring slowly up following the main channel markers from 'The Bag' down near Salcombe Town, in autumn sunshine and then sitting on the boat in the sun at the Crabshell eating scampi and sauce tartare, washed down with rosé wine.

For the serious boating man – and let's face it, for the calm water potterer – Salcombe has everything. Within minutes you can be over the Bar and in really deep, full ocean water, or if you turn inland you can sample a different kind of boating in sunlit bays and really shallow seas. So shallow, in fact, that you must watch where you are going and the state of the tide, unless you wish to play at 'African Queen' à la Humphrey Bogart and Katherine Hepburn.

I do not exaggerate when I call it a 'blue water wonderland' You can move, engine hardly turning over, through schools of grey mullet which will leap and break the still water, and on through Balcombe Bridge, which carries the road from Kingsbridge to Dartmouth, into a lake where the trees are cut off low as though with some mighty hedge-cutter. It is only when you think about it that you realise this perfectly even trimming of the lower branches is carried out by the tide, whose sea salt stops the branches growing any lower.

We have an advantage with our inflatable boat, shared with some sailing dinghies, in that it draws no more than a few inches of water. We can therefore penetrate up to such delightful pubs as the one at South Pool. It is the sort of place – something out of the past – where the landlord tells you if you ought to be going – or you will be stranded by the tide. South Pool has, in addition to a splendid pub, a fine fourteenth century church, and an ancient set of stepping-stones across the very end of the creek. There is about it an air of peace that is hard to equal.

But despite this, don't forget that you are deep in smuggling country and the war between the 'Gentlemen' and the Revenue men was fought no less fiercely here than anywhere else in this South Devon countryside. The enthusiastic Revenue man must indeed have had a hard time among these creeks and backwaters – there are so many getaways that when you glide in a boat up the Salcombe Estuary it is easy to get the idea that you are not in Britain at all but in some beautiful foreign waterworld that makes Venice look like an industrial slum, it is difficult in these watery surroundings not to get a sense of history. This was the home of the fruit clippers, which were built along the shores of the Estuary in the 1800's. In the 1860's the Kingsbridge Packet ran twice weekly from the town to Plymouth – it was quicker by water than by horse. At Balcombe Bridge, which I mentioned earlier – or rather just before it at High House Point – were the Kingsbridge town gallows. Perhaps it is not surprising that the cemetery is nearby.

They say that the Saltstone, just below the entrance to Frogmore Lake, was where, in the seventeenth century crowds would gather at low tide, to hear Non-conformist preachers. They say, too, that the islet was beyond the arm of the law. But it would seem to me that all the law had to do was to wait until the incoming tide drove these 'heretics' ashore and into their arms.

Salcombe, Kingsbridge, Hope – and probably Thurlestone – were renowned for 'white ale' in years gone by. It has long since died out as a local drink. And I think I know why. The contents were milk, spices and the main ingredient – gin. I can understand its popularity – and I have no doubt some enterprising landlord probably now either serves it, or is intending to, to the tourist trade. However, the reason for its existence as a local drink of the past was solely due to the smuggling trade. Those smugglers didn't only bring in brandy and rum, but also 'geneva' or gin. Neat gin is pretty paralytic-making. Served with milk and herbs, a little could last a long time.

Still, this is a digression. We were discussing the beauties and history of the Salcombe Estuary. Here, on the history front, I am indebted to Margaret Willy, whose splendid book, simply called *The South Hams,* was written with great affection for the area. It is now, sadly, out of the print, so you should pester the publishers, Robert Hale & Co., if you want a reprint.

Mrs Willy researched the old days of Salcombe and Kingsbridge for her book and established that the fruit clippers, which were barques, brigantines, brigs and schooners (from 100 to 550 tons) were built for a thousand seamen to man them on voyages for fruit. These voyages started from the Estuary. The ships were designed, like the famous tea clippers, for speed – to get the perishable fruit home in good condition. They bore local names — Avon, Churchstow, Erme, Alvington, Malborough, even Salcombe Castle.

'In the last half of the eighteenth century,' wrote Margaret Willy, 'after the end of the Seven Years War, Salcombe Harbour was thronged with vessels of all types and sizes. The sight of these laden ships waiting to discharge rich cargoes – West Indian cocoa, coffee and tobacco, rum, molasses, spices, arrowroot, ginger and sugar, timber and cotton from the United States, grain, meat and hides from South America, Mediterranean oils and wines, rubber, silk, and so on – had given Salcombe the real incentive for building her own shipyards and sending out local seamen to these lands of plenty. . . .

'One of the biggest and best-known yards on the estuary was at Kingsbridge : the Shipwrights' Yard, which stood near the Crabshell Inn and was, during its heyday in the 'sixties, turning out many of the old 'fruiters' . . .

'It closed down about forty years ago . . . the conquest of wood and sail by steel and steam was complete.'

Looking at the thousands of yachts, boats and humble dinghies moored in the Salcombe Estuary today, I don't suppose that anyone would agree that the conquest of sail had actually taken place! But we have not been confined – if you can possibly call it that – in our boating to the Salcombe Estuary. There are two other boating centres that intrigue us in the South Hams. One is the Yealm, the other the Avon which winds down to the sea at Bantham.

The Yealm (launch at Newton Ferrers) is, I think, just slightly more beautiful than Salcombe, but only in certain parts of the river.

Boating at Bantham can be difficult, but with care and tide you can get up to the bridge at Aveton Gifford, though you do run a great risk of getting stranded in this tidal estuary of the Avon if you don't time things right. It is odd to think of this quiet inlet being a prosperous harbour, but pilchards were landed there by the thousand and cured in a building still to be seen. A regular steamship from Plymouth to Bantham was another additional activity, as well as the transfer into barges of cargoes of coal and stone for transport further up river.

As we idled dreamily around on the historic waters of the South Hams, I wondered more and more about the age of my cottage. Would any new clues come from all the letters I had written? However, it was not the letters which brought more information, but a simple telephone call.

I had been thinking for some time that if only the beams in the cottage could talk, they could tell quite a story. And then it occurred to me that perhaps the beams could be made to talk if I could find an expert who could look at a photograph of them and say, 'Definitely fourth century, old man'. Well, it was a daft idea, but worth a telephone call. So I rang the Society for the Protection of Ancient Buildings in Great Ormond Street, London, W.C.1, and put my question.

They laughed, I laughed, but they put me through to Mrs Monica Dance. Mrs Dance laughed too. But she quickly took charge of my inquiry with professional expertise and cross-examined me about the checks I had made so far about the age of the building. It was a delight to deal with someone who not only knew what I was talking about, but immediately understood my interest.

During the course of our conversation she told me that she has an old cottage of her own. She illustrated the further inquiries I should make by telling me the things she had found out during her own research into the history of her cottage. She pointed out almost at once that if my cottage was a listed building there must be details of why it was listed. Soon she was reading out to me an extract from the 'List of Buildings of Special Architectural or Historic Interest in the Rural District of Kingsbridge and Civil Parish of Thurlestone'.

'Just-a-Cottage' was there all right. Listed as 'Grade Two' (Well, all right. Grade Two. But then Blenheim Palace is only Grade One!) Seriously, most buildings come under the Grade Two listing. But 'Just-a-Cottage' is important enough to be listed for its value when combined with the adjoining building. It is described, and I don't know that I agree with the description, as: 'Colourwash rubble with thatched roofs and brick and

Cottage past. The awful lean-to at the back of 'Just-a-Cottage'. The little window, top right, is now the window of the bathroom

Cottage present. The new kitchen, replacing the lean-to shed. The stable door is one we found there

Cottage past. The partition wall by the stairs will disappear in the conversion work; so will the asbestos sheet ceiling and (extreme right) the range and fireplace

Cottage present. The partition wall has gone. The truncheons hang by the mirror. The beams are now exposed. The dresser, before being stripped, is on the left

rubble stacks. Two stories. Casements. Five window front. Query seventeenth Century. Group value.' So the Department of the Environment when listing the building as of special architectural and/or historic interest, do consider the two cottages as one. Five window front includes not only 'Just-a-Cottage' but also Len Jeffery's cottage next door.

During my conversation with Mrs Dance, she asked me if I had deeds back to that time. I was obliged to reply that the deeds, except for the modern ones, are missing. 'Made into a lampshade', said Mrs Dance with a note of sadness in her voice, and I know exactly what she means. So often deeds of historic importance have been used for some get-rich-quick operation like making lampshades out of the parchment. All I can say here is – if by chance you switch on your table lamp and see the word 'Thurlestone' or something like it glowing near the bulb, please let me know.

It's my cottage which is lighting up your living room!

10. Bloody Murder

If you think that the whole history of Thurlestone and the surrounding area is one of peaceful happy folk, smiling their way through the centuries, then I'm afraid that this chapter will come as something of a shock. Thurlestone was no different from the rest of England in days gone by. The sort of barbarity and cruelty that would totally shock us today was commonplace even in those lazy, winding Devon lanes. And nowhere was this more apparent than in the places where the sea touched the shore.

For the sea was the bringer of plenty – fish and food, those came by honest labour. But there was another kind of plenty – the stricken ship and cargo for looting. Heaven help the man who got in the way of such sudden wealth! It is true to say that more ships have been wrecked around the coasts of Britain than the shores of any other country in the world. We have always been an island with difficult coasts to weather.

And if our local sailors knew the danger spots, the ships of other nations which came to trade with us did not. As a result, the details of recorded wrecks over the centuries would take an entire library to house. The number of unrecorded ones – save only by the grave of an unknown sailor – cannot even be guessed at.

As a diver, the history of wrecks has always been one of my great interests. In writing books about wrecks* I have dived on and found, I have collected just as much information about those I have dived for and failed to find. Research has taken me from Public Record Office to church graveyard, from one line in an ancient history book to oldest inhabitant, and from one word from oldest inhabitant to correspondence with the keepers of archives all over Europe and the United States of America.

Every time that research has turned up the word 'Devon' my

**The Wreck Hunters; The Wreck Detectives* both published by George G. Harrap & Co Ltd.

senses have given that extra twitch. But the picture that has usually emerged is not one of smiling faces lining the shore to aid the stricken sailor. Far from it.

Take the last voyage of a brig called 'Chantiloupe'. She was coming back from the West Indies in 1772 and having survived the major part of the voyage, all aboard thought that their troubles were over. But if she was making for Plymouth, she had desperately overshot the mark. If she was making for ports further up the Channel, she had still a way to go when a South-Westerly gale picked her up and drove her towards the shore.

That shore was Thurlestone Sands. Whether the captain saw the unmistakable outline of Thurlestone Rock in his last moments we do not know. By then he was totally committed to running the ship ashore to save what he could. It would, perhaps, have been better if the bottom had been ripped out of his ship on some headland further down the Channel. For, though of course no one on board could know it, they were all to die – and one of them was to be murdered in a particularly ghastly manner.

There is no evidence that I can find to explain the beaching of the ship on Thurlestone Sands. But even so there can be only one reason. Once inside Bigbury Bay and under the lee of Bolt Tail, the Captain, with a South-Westerly gale behind him, had no chance of beating his way out to the open sea. He could anchor – and hope to ride it out. But we don't know if he had any anchors left. Maybe he had tried that and lost them. Cables and anchors in those days were not able to stand up to the same sort of strain that much smaller anchors and nylon ropes can take today.

If you stand, or try to stand, on Thurlestone Sands in a South-Westerly gale in winter today, you will see the spray flowing like a river flood across the bay. If you see, too, the spume blowing high above the Rock, you will have some idea of the impossible conditions that captain had to face.

Did the captain catch a glimpse of Thurlestone Rock during a gap in the driven walls of water? I don't know, but I do know that by the time he made his final run for the beach all on board were doomed. The crash, the striking, the slewing, the lurch, and then finally the almost complete capsize that poured salt-water into the lungs of passenger and crew alike can only be imagined. But not all went at that first shock. Not all died as the water swept across the deck.

There is evidence to suggest that the passengers had been aware for some time that they were bound to be wrecked. For Mrs Burke, one of the passengers and a relation of parliamentarian orator Edmund Burke, had seen fit to put on her jewellery – rings, earrings, and possibly even all the necklaces from her vanity boxes. This suggests an intention to get ashore with all the valuables that she could.

Some reports of the wreck suggest that one man survived; I doubt it. But I am sure that Mrs Burke reached the shore alive. Whether she was washed up floating, or whether she waded unaided out of the surf, the result of her endeavours was the same. She was seized, not by helping hands, but by those whose only thought was loot. They fought over her as they tore the earrings from her ears. And when they could not get the rings from her sea-swollen fingers, they cut them off to get at the gems.

There is a story that no one realised that she was alive until the blood ran from her fingers as they hacked away. But it doesn't ring true. They killed her for those valuables. For the same reason, it is not likely to be true that one man survived the wreck. After such butchery, would one man have been allowed to remain alive to tell the tale? No, they buried Mrs Burke in the sand and their brutality would have remained the secret of those who had gone beserk in the blood-stained surf had it not been for a dog.

All we know about the dog is that he was owned by the father of a local called Jan Whiddon, a name which in itself raises more than faint echoes of 'Old Uncle Tom Cobleigh and All'. Mr Whiddon took his dog with him when he went along the beach and that dog dug up the mutilated body of Mrs Burke. At the inquest it was proved that she was still alive when she reached shore, but no more than that. A Mrs Ilbert (a good Devon and Thurlestone name, that) had the body buried in a proper Christian manner and it would seem that that was as far as the matter went. It is said that Edmund Burke came down to investigate what had happened to his relative, but nothing could be tighter than a group of guilty countrymen and he learned nothing which could lead to a prosecution. No one would talk to a 'foreigner' – a name about which retired settlers in Devon should not take umbrage; after all even Cornishmen are 'foreigners' to the Devonians who live just across Plymouth Sound!

But memories in the country are long. And, though it sounds incredible, the Reverend Frank Egerton Coope,* who was Rector of Thurlestone from 1897 to 1921, wrote in his valuable book *Thurlestone Church and Parish,* published during that time, that 'it was well-known in the neighbourhood who did it, and their surnames are remembered to this day'!

He added that the three men most concerned in the murder all, so local gossip had it, came 'to a bad end' – one hanged himself in an outhouse; one was killed in an accident; and the third went mad and ran into the sea and was drowned. It all sounds too neat an ending for a bloody murder and wreck that it is impossible to imagine when sitting in the sun on Thurlestone Sands today.

But it would be wrong to think that the looting of wrecks in Thurlestone and district started then. It had been going on for years, even centuries.

One of my sources for such a statement is once again a man of God. Henry Hingeston was a Quaker, a merchant in Kingsbridge and he lived from 1668 to 1724. He got very cross about the loose-living of the inhabitants of Kingsbridge and those who lived round about. So he wrote, in 1703, what amounts to a lecture to them which he entitled, 'A Dreadful Alarm upon the Clouds of Heaven Mixed With Love'. Anyone might be forgiven for thinking this was a work of theology, but the first part soon destroys this illusion. It is an 'Address to England, Containing Sundry Warnings and admonitions to the Inhabitants Thereof, More Particularly to those of the Town of Kingsbridge, in Devon (the Place of my Nativity and Abode) and Parts Adjacent'.

*The Reverend Frank Egerton Coope left Thurlestone and in 1922 took up the living of Danehill in the Ashdown Forest in Sussex. Mr Coope had eleven children. One of them, Mrs Clare Tottenham, who now lives in Putney, London, tells me that her father retired to Haywards Heath, Sussex, but died on holiday in Palermo, Sicily, on March 13th, 1934. He is buried there.

There is no doubt that Henry Hingeston was pretty cross with them. Under a heading of 'Wrack', he wrote:

'I have also been deeply affected to see and feel how sweet the Report of a Shipwrack is to the Inhabitants of this Country, as well Professors as Profane; and what running there is on such Occasions, all other business thrown aside, and away to Wrack.

'Hearken a little: Suppose you were Cast away in a strange country, having much to do to save your Lives, but however you come safe ashore, and are in some Capacity of saving most, if not all your Goods, by some small assistance; but at the same time, to prevent you from that, down comes a Parcel of Fellows on you, that instead of Helping of you, take away all, and compassionate you no more than Dogs, nay, if you have sav'd anything, they'll be forward to take it from you; but when they cannot do that, you being driven of Necessity to sell, they'll scarce give half, perhaps not a quarter its value. Pray what would you say of those folks? Well, then, pray look home and examine the Constitution of this Country; have you not done as bad as all this?

'I conclude you cannot say no, except against your Knowledge. Nay, have you not done much worse? I say you have. Remember the Broad-Cloth Slupe stranded in Bigbury Bay. Richly laden.'

It is quite obvious that Henry Hingeston had suffered badly at the hands of looters, and one suspects that he had a large interest in the Bigbury Bay sloop.

He was not the first to suffer so. Not by a long way. But before you condemn those who looted what they looked upon as free gifts from the sea, you should try and imagine the near starvation-level standard of living which the bounty from a wreck could raise, literally overnight at least to a certainty of full bellies for years. So the message flew from village to village of a ship in trouble. And the people came to the shore, perhaps to help save life – provided that did not get in the way of the loot.

My fellow-diver, Richard Larn, is one of the finest chroniclers of wrecks in Britain today. Writing about this aspect of wrecks – admittedly he was referring to Cornwall* – he puts it like this:

'A rumour of goods for the taking was enough to bring people from all walks of life hurrying to a wreck. As if by magic, donkey

**Cornish Shipwrecks: The South Coast* (David and Charles Ltd).

carts, hand-carts, even wheelbarrows would appear, be loaded to overflowing, and then as quickly disappear. Goods were buried on clifftops for subsequent recovery, hidden in mill-ponds and under water-wheels, beneath cottage flagstones, or in the thatch, or – a favourite place – in mine shafts.'

The truth is that plundering wrecks was considered by the inhabitants to be a West Country right. Daniel Defoe of *Robinson Crusoe* fame wrote during a visit to the West Country in 1724 of 'the sands covered in people, they are charged with strange bloody and cruel dealings, even sometimes with one another, but especially with poor distressed seamen who seek for help for their lives and find the rocks themselves not more cruel and merciless than the people who range about them for their prey'.

However, the law did not turn a blind eye to this as they tended to do with smuggling. The right of wreck was worth a lot of money. The lords of the manor of 'Thurlstone' must therefore have thought it quite a windfall when, on October 12th, 1340, Edward III awarded them the right to unclaimed wreckage between Dartmouth Castle and Bantham.

Unfortunately, from the sailor's point of view, the laws of unclaimed wreck were an incitement to murder him as he staggered ashore. Here are those rules for dealing with a wreck in the Thurlestone area: 'Whosoever finds any wrecked goods ought to carry it to the chief inhabitants of the town or place next to where it was found, and there to remain until a claim be made to it, either by any person saved alive belonging to the ship, or their wives, children, or executors, owner, merchant, or such a good title to the land.

'And if no claim be made with a year and a day, then it must be delivered to the Admiral, or such as hath the Royal privilege of the Royalty, paying reasonable for their trouble for salvage.

'If any man or living thing escape to shore alive, it is no wreck.

'If any one should have a lanthorne or make a light in order to subject them in danger of shipwreck (if no harm happen), yet it is a felony.

'If anyone convey secretly any of the goods, if it be the value of a nail, it is felony.

'If any cast out any ballast from any ship or boat with the

port of Salcombe contrary to the statute forfeits 3s 4d. If it be let lie there forty-eight hours, shall forfeit 40s.

'If anyone doth labour within this Royalty between sun and sun on the Sabbath-day forfeits 40s.

'If anyone ashore salt pilchards, and suffer the guts to be thrown, or go into the salt water forfeits for each offence 3s 4d.'

The last clauses hardly apply to wreck, but they do give some idea of the ideas prevailing in these times. The vital clause is the one that says that 'if any man or living thing escape to shore alive, it is no wreck'.

If he made sure that no man or woman or cat or dog did reach the beach alive, the salvor, even if caught with the goods, did stand a chance of saying that he was merely taking it 'to the chief inhabitants of the town or the place next to where it was found' and could make some sort of claim for salvage.

I must say, that in addition to this invitation to murder, I find the reference to luring a ship into danger by means of lights an odd one. Everyone says that this did go on. And many a British novel or Hollywood film has been based on it. Yet the evidence that it did take place is obvious by its absence. There are two theories which can account for this. One is that there were enough shipwrecks without false lights to make it unnecessary.

The second theory is that so tight was the Devon code of silence in those days – a sort of Modbury Mafia? – that, in the South Hams at least, no one was ever found to give evidence of deliberate wrecking. However, commonsense would seem to say that such a clause would not have been laid down if wrecking did not, or had not, taken place.

Of the looting of ships which came ashore without the assistance of wreckers there is plenty of evidence. One of the earliest on record is of a hospital ship of the Spanish Armada. She met her end on the Shippen Rock in Hope Cove. And was plundered with added zest because she was Spanish.

But her agony had started long before these last moments. She was called *San Pedro el Mayor.* In the Armada records she belonged in squadron of urcas, or hulks. These were cargo-carrying vessels of all kinds which had been pressed into service as store and supply ships.

This squadron of hulks, according to an inventory made in

Lisbon on May 20th, 1588, had fourteen ships in it. They were all cumbersome, and could only make slow speed compared with the Armada's fighting ships. The hospital ship, *San Pedro el Mayor,* was no exception. She was of medium size, 550 tons burden, and had left Spain with thirty sailors and a hundred soldiers – fifty men-at-arms to fight on land or repel boarders and fifty others whose rôle was to tend the sick and organise the hospital on board.

She was off Plymouth with the rest of the Armada on July 21st, 1588, when the first skirmishes took place with the English ships, carrying such legendary names as Howard, Drake, Hawkins and Frobisher. They were only skirmishes and Drake recorded it as such: 'The 21st we had them in chase, and so, coming up to them, there hath passed some cannon shot between some of our fleet and some of them, and as far as we perceive, they are determined to sell their lives with blows'.

Just how many were to sell their lives even Drake, at that time, could have no conception – it would have passed his wildest dreams. The story of the Armada is too well told to go into it fully here. But the story of the *San Pedro* is not so well known. Three months later she was to appear at almost the same spot off Plymouth, but in very different circumstances.

As the battles increased so did the number of wounded transferred to her hospital. Nine days later, when the fleet should have been moving victoriously up the Thames and the *San Pedro* should have been able to put her patients ashore, the real voyage of the Armada was only just beginning.

On July 30th, 1588, the Armada was about twenty miles west of Flushing and the entrance to the river Sheldt, heading North-North-East towards Norway. English cannon had begun the work – one Armada ship is described as having blood running out of her into the sea – and now the weather was taking over. North went the Armada and the *San Pedro* lurched after them. The wounded began to die. Disease, hunger and seasickness added to the death roll.

So the Duke of Medina Sidonia, commanding the Armada from his flagship the *San Martin de Portugal,* took what was left of his fleet to the West between the Orkneys and the Shetlands – and lost some ships on those stormy shores – before turning South for Spain. He ventured a long way out from the

Irish coast as he feared that any ship luckless enough to have to touch Ireland would meet with no quarter. All his captains were commanded not to seek shelter in Irish ports. Some did, despite these orders, because they could not help themselves and Armada wrecks in Irish waters were plentiful to say the least.

There is some evidence that the *San Pedro el Mayor* did venture into the port of Vicey, County Kerry, to try and pick up fresh water and get a day or two's shelter from the endless foul weather. This call for fresh water was sometime around September 20th, 1588. The mere fact that the Captain was prepared to risk entering an Irish port, despite his Admiral's orders not to do so, gives us some idea of the conditions on board.

The *San Pedro el Mayor* was soon off again – into the teeth of more westerly gales. But her ability to weather such storms was going fast. Fewer and fewer men were available to man the ship. And God knows what was happening to the sick and wounded down below.

At the end of October the *San Pedro el Mayor* was back almost exactly where she had been three months previously – off Plymouth – having circumnavigated the British Isles. There were not enough men left on their feet to handle her properly. A South-Westerly gale picked her up and blew her along until she was heading straight in into the nest of her enemies, Plymouth. But then the wind shifted a little, or maybe the crew desperately got a little canvas on her. If they did, it didn't help. She came into Bigbury Bay and then, as though bent on suicide, straight into Hope Cove. And there on the Shippen Rock at the beginning of November, 1588, her miserable voyage ended. Soon she was a complete wreck and the pillaging began.

You'll find the evidence that pillaging took place a long way from Hope Cove – in the Public Record Office in Chancery Lane, London among the Calendar of State Papers for 1588. In this collection are all manner of reports and letters concerning the Armada campaign. Two are of great interest and concern the wreck at Hope almost exclusively.

The first comes from a man whose account ought to be trusted completely. George Cary, a Deputy-Lieutenant of Devon, was in Plymouth when he heard of the wreck and rode posthaste to the scene. In his letter, dated November 5th, 1588, he put it like this:

'And during my abode there, having understanding that one of the Spanish fleet was cast on shore (at a place called Hope near Salcombe) and the great pilfering and spoils that the country people made, I rode thither and took order for the restoring and rehaving again of all such things as either by search or inquiry I could find out, and have put the same in inventory. And took order, for the orderly saving of the rest, as weather would give leave, to have the same on land, appointing two head constables to attend that service, and they and others to keep several inventories.

'The ship is a hulk, and called St. Peter the Great, one of those two ships which were appointed for the hospital of the whole Navy. She is in burden, as they say, 550 tons, but I think not so much.

'The ship is not to be recovered; she lieth on a rock, and full of water to her upper decks. They confess that there were put into her, at her coming out of Spain, thirty mariners, one hundred soldiers, fifty appertaining to the hospital. There are now remaining about forty, or thereabouts.'

If this is a true report of her complement at the time of her wrecking, it is a staggering statement. It indicates only too clearly the agony and the hell that the *San Pedro el Mayor* had gone through on her three-month voyage. Two-thirds of those who had joined her in the joyous setting out from Spain had gone – and that doesn't even take account of the wounded transferred to her during the battles up the Channel three months before or during her circumnavigation of Britain. But Cary had not finished his description of what had happened at Hope:

'There was put into her as much drugs and pothecary stuff as came to 6,000 ducats, of which I think there will come little good of the same, the weather such as none could get aboard. There hath been some plate and certain ducats rifled and spoiled at their first landing, both from their persons and out of their chests. The ship, I think, will prove of no great value; the ordnance is all iron and no brass; their ground tackle all spent, save only one new cable.

He concludes after that further indication of the struggle of the *San Pedro* – they had used up all their anchors and cables, presumably trying to avoid being cast ashore somewhere else – that 'there are no men of account in the ship, soldiers and such as have risen by service, and bestowed all their wealth in this action'.

It is quite clear by this last sentence including such damning phrases as 'no men of account' that Cary was thinking once again of the value of the wreck. Men of no account would mean that they were not worth ransom. But before we condemn the mercenary – on the Queen's behalf – Mr Cary we should know that while ten of the prisoners were sent into Kingsbridge, the apothecary and surgeon of the ship were looked after by Cary himself at his home in Cockington. Eight were sent to Ilton Castle in charge of Sir William Courtenay, who was the third Earl of Devon and High Sheriff of Devonshire.

It is perhaps ironic that after Sir Francis Drake's death, the man who had looked after some of the *San Pedro's* prisoners – they were after all partially the result of Drake's harassing of the Armada up the Channel – that same man, Sir William Courtenay, a widower with a large family, should have married the wealthy and handsome widow, Lady Drake in 1597 (Captain, art thou sleeping there below?).

Cary, for all his care about money, seems to have been a humane man. He assigned to each prisoner out of his own private purse one penny per day until the pleasure of Her Majesty's Privy Council – to whom he had addressed his letter with its account of the wrecking – should be made known.

I cannot imagine that apart from this the prisoners were treated with much care. According to the Archives Nationales, Paris, K. 1592 (Dossier B.81), one of the Kingsbridge prisoners was interrogated on November 7th, 1588.

In his statement, Gonzalo Gonzalez said: 'The hulk *San Pedro el Mayor* of the squadron of Juan Gomez de Medina was cast ashore in England, on the land of Sir William Courtenay, where she was pillaged and her people imprisoned'. It is no surprise to find that people like Señor Gonzales were prepared to talk – shortly after their capture orders were given for them to be executed, but these orders were later countermanded. Presumably only after they had told all they knew.

The second letter to the Privy Council – also in the Public

Record Office – is from Anthony Ashley, who was clerk to the Privy Council. He seems to have moved to Ilton Castle shortly after the news of the wreck reached London, and his letter, dated November 12th, is from Ilton: 'May it please your Lordships, the ship being run upon rocks by the Spaniards, is now through the tempestuous weather broken in pieces and scattered on the seashore, and order is taken for the saving of such things as are anything worth.'

So there it is. A period of uncontrolled looting, followed by the arrival of Cary and his constables, followed by a storm that ripped what was left of the wreck apart and dumped it on the seashore. I said earlier on that my interest in wrecks was that of a diver. One would think that there would be some trace of the *San Pedro el Mayor* on the seabed around Hope. I have dived there myself and found nothing. One local diver did report finding old ship's timbers on the bottom, but could not relocate them after a storm.

If you go into the saloon bar of the Thurlestone Inn you will see there beams that are without doubt, ship's timbers. They are said to be from the *San Pedro el Mayor* – and I see no reason to doubt that. But the story does not end there. The amateur divers of the British Sub-Aqua Club are not easily put off and they go on diving the Hope site. What is puzzling is that underwater there are no traces of ancient hospital equipment, not even the odd pestle or mortar. You would think there would be some trace – even a cracked chip of an old bottle – but the divers can find nothing. Each fine weekend they go on trying and if you look down from the cliff-tops after walking from Thurlestone Sands to Hope, and see divers in the froth around the Shippen Rock, that is what they are seeking.

You see there is shore-bound evidence of the wreck. Every now and then – particularly after a North-East blow when the under-surface of Inner Hope beach is exposed and the stiff clay base shows again – coins are found. And these coins are about the size of a half-crown and bear on one side the Maltese cross and on the other the Spanish arms surmounted with the royal crown. Some have the name of Philip, worn but clear.

This, to me, is clear evidence, not only of the wreck, but of the looting that went on as soon as the *San Pedro* came ashore. During the frenzy of looting some coins were lost, stamped into the beach and forgotten. I believe that it is these coins which come to light every now and then today.

That is the story of the *San Pedro el Mayor*. It is the story of looting and of wreck. But she was by no means the only ship to come to grief on these shores – and by no means the last to be looted.

11. Wreck, Wreck, Wreck!

Perhaps you think that I am being too hard on the ancestors of the delightful people who live today in Thurlestone, Hope, Buckland, Bigbury – in fact, in all the villages of the South Hams. If you do, you are making a mistake. I am not condemning those people of days long ago, but merely drawing your attention to the appalling conditions under which they had to live – it was those conditions that drove them to think of every wrecked ship as a gift from Heaven.

It was a world that is difficult to imagine in today's comfortable setting. Can you imagine what sort of life would lead people to board a ship wrecked in the 1600's, find there a Roman Catholic priest, lock him up and send for the local hound pack to hunt him across the seashore and the fields? It was a world of superstition, poverty, misery and unbelievable ignorance. The people who made the priest their prisoner and intended to have sport with him as the quarry of the Malborough hounds, believed that he had come to conspire against their Government, just as the Armada had come to turn them all into Catholic slaves.

Fortunately, in this case, the priest was saved from a horrible stumbling, dog-torn death by the intervention of 'some local gentry'. But the mere fact that he was saved from the actual tearing to pieces doesn't conceal the fact that this is what was intended.

The truth is that so valuable to the ordinary people of Devon was a wreck that when a sailing ship was caught inshore with an onshore wind, people would gather from miles around to watch the ship beating about in the bay. The ship's last agony could take days and the crowds would move along the coast as the ship moved back and forth attempting to claw her way to the open sea. It seems incredible today that these crowds of onlookers – well, one could hardly describe them as well-wishers – would be numbered in thousands. That is some indication of the wealth that a 'good' wreck could bring to people close to the monetary starvation line.

Does the idea of thousands of people gathering on Thurlestone Sands surprise you? Listen then to the words of Mr George Taylor to Sir William Courtenay on January 16th, 1753. He was in Totnes when he wrote this letter.

Honoured Sir,

'I hope you, my lady and family, had a safe journey to Town, after such bad weather, as probably you had on your road.

'I'm to acquaint you that last Wednesday night, about ten, a Hamburgh-Dutch galliott, burden about one hundred tons, laden with wine, brandy, coffee, indigo, and one bale of saffron, bound from Zante to Hamburgh, was stranded on Thurlestone sands, within the precincts of your Royalty.

'Thursday morn I went thither to do what lay in my power to prevent the country from plundering her and to save the cargo, and have the pleasure to let your honour know that more than three parts of four is so done.

'The lost cable and anchor I've secured (as usual) for your use; but as to what share of the salvage (extracted from the expenses of saving) is due to you I'm at a loss to judge at, especially as the ship is not broke to pieces by the waves, and the master and men all saved, and not deemed wreck.

'As your Honour is in Town you may advise what is most proper to be done by me for your interest. The Custom House officers of Plymouth, Dartmouth, and Salcombe all assisted in saving the goods. The cargo is valued at about £3,000. A great part of the goods are in the custody of Mr Adams and others of your tenants.

'A great part of the goods were saved Thursday and Friday from being plundered by my being there, on account of my acquaintance and knowing most of the persons then there; but Saturday evening there were not less than ten thousand people who came from remote parts in order to plunder the remainder of the cargo, which they had certainly done if the Plymouth official had not ordered a party of soldiers to attend, who opportunely came just as the mob was about to make a disturbance; by accident one of the ringleaders was killed, he being drunk and falling upon one of the soldier's bayonets fixed on the

Thurlestone in the Great Blizzard of 1891 Dartington Rural Archives

Thatching the cottage. David Trant uses his bat to drive the new thatch home. The discarded straw is already piling up over downstairs windows

The S.S. Jebba, *aground in 1907. All 155 passengers were saved, being taken off by breeches-buoy from the cliffs above Soar Mill Cove*

The Louis Shied, *the ship which went ashore almost on Thurlestone Golf Course in 1939. Thurlestone Hotel is on the right*

gun. This and other circumstances gave a damp to the rest of the rioters; and more goods have been saved out of this vessel than all the ships that have been stranded for fifty years past.

I am, your Honour's most faithful servant,

Geo. Taylor

P.S. I'm but just come home weary and tired, wet every day into the skin, but helping the distressed makes an atonement.'

I think the letter says it all – even allowing for George Taylor's toadying attitude to Sir William. It is interesting to note that as you delve into the history of wrecks, such letters become commonplace. This postscript matches many others. The agent was always keen to stress the misery he, personally, has gone through while about his Master's business.

For such a placid smiling coast – in summer – the number of ships which have to come to grief in this area over the centuries is extraordinary. Yet if you walk from Salcombe to Hope and on to Thurlestone – quite a haul and not one to be attempted with young children – you will be bound to capture some of the feeling of desolation of that great area of National Trust land when you look down from stark cliffs to the jagged sea-spittled black tongues of rock hundreds of feet below. There is not much hope for a disabled engined-craft of today caught close-in to those five miles of cliffs by any on-shore wind. Imagine, then, what little chance there was for ships in similar circumstances long ago if they had to rely on sail to pull them clear. The evidence that so many failed to make it out to sea and safety can be found in every village churchyard in the area.

Look, for example, in the churchyard at Malborough. There you will find a memorial to three boys and a girl, all from the same family, who died when the homeward-bound *Dragon* from Jamaica to London, smashed into the rocks at Cathole on August 23rd, 1757 in a South West gale*

Cathole Cliffs are not far from Soar Mill Cove and a worse place to be wrecked it is difficult to imagine. The surprising thing about this wreck is that even in those circumstances Cap-

*The inscription on the gravestone reads: 'Here lye the bodies of Rhodes, Daniel, Mary and Joseph Chambers, sons and daughters of Edward Chambers, of Jamaica, who were shipwrecked at Cat-hole, within this parish, August 22nd, 1757.'

tain Edward Gleast and ten men of his crew were saved. Reports of the number drowned vary, but a search of the Burney Collection of newspapers in the British Museum for the week following August 22nd 1757, revealed that the *Public Advertiser* of August 30th, 1757, the *London Chronicle* for August 27th-30th, 1757, and *Lloyd's Evening Post and British Chronicle* for August 29th-31st, 1757, all carried a record of the wreck. But I must thank Miss Alison Gould of the British Museum staff for continuing the search.

She found that the *London Chronicle* for August 30th – September 1st, 1757 carried a longer notice of the wreck: 'They write from Dartmouth, that on the 23rd past, at eight o'clock at night, was driven ashore, little to the westward of Salcomb, and soon after beat to pieces, the Dragon, of and for London, Captain Edward Gleast, from Jamaica, laden with rum, sugar, etc., and of all the cargo only one cask of rum saved. The Captain and ten men were saved, and seven men and one boy and one girl were drowned; among whom were Mr Chambers, a planter of Jamaica, his sister and cousin.'

And Miss Gould discovered too that the *Lloyd's Evening Post and British Chronicle* for August 26th-29th, 1757 carried this report: 'It is reported, that Tuesday night was lost nigh Salcomb, a ship from Jamaica for London. The ship and cargo entirely lost, and seven of the crew, and a passenger drowned. She came out with the convoy, but passed in a gale of wind, and said a privateer had taken ten of them. I send you this but by report of a person come from Salcomb. Wind hard at S.W.'

The reference to a convoy is due to the fact that the Seven Years' War had started in 1755, so the privateer was therefore undoubtedly French. The *Dragon* was not the only loss, of course. I have a note of a ship, believed to be Dutch, that was wrecked in 1738 and then plundered locally. This could be the *Lintor Ken,* which is said to have carried a cargo of walnut wood and marble statues and to have provided local building materials for some time. But I can find no proper records.

One of the most active of local divers is Mr Bob Page, who runs the excellent Kingsbridge Watersports from a shop in Fore Street, Kingsbridge. He has searched for the *Dragon* and he believes that the absence of traces of her is due, not to the smashing of the wreckage by the sea, but the fact that there have been numerous huge cliff falls in the area, bringing down thousands of tons of rock on to the seabed close inshore.

As you search through old records, particularly those of courts-martial – and every Royal Navy ship and the surviving officer featured in one if she had been lost, wrecked, or scandalously handled – the same names crop up again and again.

After a time you can almost see the scene through those names – the quill pen of the clerk of the court-martial squeaking down every word that was said in the great cabin of some eighteenth century man-of-war. The President of the Court was usually an Admiral and there with him, gathered to judge, were the Captains – men of great experience, whose verdict meant, literally, life or death. Remember in those days you could be hung for stealing a small thing like a coil of rope – and I have seen records where the death penalty was passed for even less.

In my research I came time and time again upon the name of the Honorable Edward Boscawen. Boscawen was a survivor. A man who had been through the mill of the Navy and emerged as a stern, but not unkindly, man, an odd-mixture of sea-dog and scholar. Before setting off on some hazardous voyage he would write to his wife eloquent letters which contained such phrases as 'To be sure I lose the fruits of the earth, but then I am gathering the flowers of the sea'.

Boscawen had seen it all. But a loss of one of his ships never failed to shock him. And one of his ships was lost on February 14th, 1760, in a cove just round Bolt Tail from Hope that will be forever Ramillies.

H.M.S. Ramillies, a ninety-gun second-rate ship of the line, was old. The only reason she was at sea at all was the war with the French. In fact, she needed a major refit. The French had been defeated by Admiral Lord Hawke at Quiberon Bay in November, 1759. But the French had lost a battle, not the war, and the Royal Navy needed a blockading force in the Channel to make sure that they did not challenge once again.

That blockading force was sent out under the command of Admiral of the Blue, Edward Boscawen, His orders were to take a small flotilla and stand guard at Quiberon Bay. He set sail in January, 1760 and immediately ran into heavy weather – so heavy that he was forced to shelter at Spithead. He was storm-bound there until February 6th, then got as far as Plymouth before having to shelter once more.

His vessels were battered and tattered from the storms of the Channel. He wanted to press on, but the weather forced him to wait. And as time went on, he was told that *H.M.S. Ramillies* was missing. Hours passed – no *Ramillies*. In his heart he must have known that she was lost, but it wasn't until nearly a day later that his suspicions were confirmed. And on February 17th, 1760, he had to write this letter to the Admiralty from the *Royal William* in Plymouth Sound:

Sirs,

'I have received their Lordships' order of the 6th instant relating to the number of ships, frigates, and sloops which I am to keep under my command and shall take particular care to comply therewith.

'Yesterday I sent Mr Hall, one of the Master Attendants here, to Salcomb in order to obtain what particulars he can of the Ramillies, and to secure what men are saved, so soon as he returns shall send his report to their Lordships.

I am,
Sir,
your most obedient,
Humble servant,
E. BOSCAWEN.'

Though Admiral Boscawen had sent his man to Salcombe, the wreck was in fact much closer to Hope. Another two days went by before he was able to forward Hall's report and an account from the Customs men at Hope on to their Lordships in London. Hall's report of the state of the wreck came in the form of a letter to Boscawen. The contents were dismal enough, but it did not really spell out the extent of the disaster. In fact, some 700 men had died; only 26 were saved. Hall wrote from Thurlestone on February 17th 1760, and he got Bolt Head and Bolt Tail mixed up. This is what he told Boscawen:

THURLESTONE,
February 17-1760.

'Honourable Sir,

At one this afternoon I gott to the place where the ship was lost which is a litel to the Eastward of the Bolt Head in the dismal spot that fate designed her – She is intireley under water and what comes from her no boat can ventur to save yet as the sea is very high but as the wind is at N.W. hope tomorrow at low water to take up all the Ironwork and gather things that comes on shore and give it to the care of the officers of the Customs I cant see aney part of her, mast sails or yards soe I think the sea has split and torn them to pieces without they lay in coves that I cant see without a boat – this evening I went to the village where some of the seamen was that was saved and told them the Admirals orders they that are able gave me there word of coming to Dartm. tomorrow and those that are lame ask me how there landlords is to be paid to that I can give no answer – Sir I hope what I shale doe tomorrow will meet with your aprobation to sound in her as the guns is faling in her hole and the Fishermen told me at low water its three fathom I shale take wot step I can to preserve all the stores I can and waite your Honble Command.

'I am Sir your most obedient Humble servant to command

BENJ. HALL'

Together with Hall's letter was a report from the Hope Customs men, Frank Shepherd and Thomas Barriball, who had been on watch when the wreck took place. They said that they would be able to organise a party of eighteen men to hoist what could be saved up the cliffs.

On February 21st, 1760, Boscawen was finally able to forward a draft report of the last moments of the *Ramillies* to the Admiralty. It is largely based on details given, of course, by the twenty-six survivors. The Captain of the *Ramillies,* Captain Wittewronge Taylor, was lost with the other 600 men. Here is Boscawen's report:

'On Thursday, 14th instant in the close of the evening the Ramillies being in company with the Admiral, observed the Admiral to lower his main topsail, but could not see whether it was taken in. However, Captain Taylor ordered his to be lowered and as soon as it was dark, furled it. The ship then making much water, having sprung a leak under the larboard entering-port. William Wise imagined a butt to have started near the place. As soon as the main topsail was handed, Capt. Taylor ordered guns to be unshotted and signal lights to get ready for making the signal of Distress; – but on consultation concluded it would be better to bear away without making the signal of distress as some other of the squadron might take it to be the Admiral. They were now employed at all the pumps and buckets and hawled the main sail up and bore away under a foresail.

'About ten or eleven in the morning steering about E by N, some of the officers thought they saw the land, but the weather was so extream thick that few believed it to be the land. The master not convinced it was the land stood in to make it; got their larboard Fore-tack to the cat head and set the mainsail; about eleven they saw the land, and the master seeing Burrow Island which lays in Bigberry Bay took it for the Loo Island, and concluded they were to the westward of Plymouth.

'About this time the people on shore saw the ship, and as they say, she was rather to the northward of the Bolt, and were in hopes that she would have brought up in Bigberry Bay rather than attempt to weather the Bolt, as a very great swell set right on it; but to their surprize they saw her wear, and get their starboard tacks on board and set their topsails.

'They now endeavoured to weather the Eastermost Point, taking it for the Ramhead; set the courses and close reef'd topsails: The Captain, as well as some other Officers, said they could not weather the land; the Master was persuaded they could, but soon saw his mistake, and endeavoured to stay the ship and get into Bigberry Bay; but the great swell, together with her having much water in her hold would not admit of it.

'At this time Wm. Wise and Robuck were standing by the Main sheet; they heard sombody say the mainmast is sprung; and presently they heard the Captain call, "Let go the Mainsheet". Which they did and ran directly upon deck, where they found the Main mast gone and presently the Mizon mast – Wise then heard the Master call, "Let go the anchor and clew up forward", which was done; they then let go another anchor and cut away their foremast, which carried the Bowsprit with it; this was about two o'clock, and the ship about a quarter of a mile from the Bolt's Tail, but the weather was so thick that as yet they not know the land. She rode till the dusk of the evening when she drove; they then let go the sheet anchor, but before they could give her cable to bring up, she struck with her starboard quarter, and her bow then drove to the westward and took the rocks.

'William Wise who seems to be clear in his account, says that he was the last man that jumped on shore; he let loose the starboard stern ladder, and went down it, and threw himself on the rocks where the ship fell upon his right leg and bruised it to pieces, but that he got up in that condition and looked back, and could not see any more of the ship – The stem is drove into a cave to the eastward, where she struck and most of the men lay in the surf of that cave; but the ship drove to such small pieces that it appears like piles of firewood. – One of her cables lays over a rock and seems to have hold of the bow of her, but it is impossible to be certain where her bottom lays until fine weather admits of boats making a stricter survey.'

Boscawen signed that report and it seems pretty clear. Clear indication also of the poor state of navigation of the ship. The main cause of the tragedy is undoubtedly the fact that the Captain, Master and crew all thought that they were still to the west of Plymouth. To mistake Burgh Island for Looe Island was the crux of the disaster. I think it fair to say that more nonsense has been talked and written about the *Ramillies* tragedy than almost any other Navy wreck in history.

For example, Captain Wittewronge Taylor, the captain of *Ramillies,* had a reputation for being a hard man. There is no evidence that he was any harder than other captains in a Navy where hard men thrived. And the story that there was a seaman on board at the time of her loss, who came from Bigbury and had been pressed into service also seems to have no basis in fact. The story goes that this seaman recognised Bolt Tail when everyone else thought it was Rame Head and when he reported this to the captain was clapped in irons for insubordination. The story just will not stand up to examination.

After the wreck a poem called 'Shipwreck' was composed – it is said to be by William Falconer, who was the surviving midshipman, but his name does not appear on the pay-books of *Ramillies.* It was pretty graphic stuff:

Seven hundred and twenty brave men had she,
And ninety good guns to keep her company,
In a few minutes after with a most dreadful shock,
Oh, the fatal Ramillies, she dashed upon a rock.'

It doesn't fit at all. The number of crew is wrong, so are the number of guns, which, by the way, were nearly all salvaged after the wreck.

I am not going to go into the intricacies of buying a Naval wreck. That is dealt with in other books – suffice it to say here that the *Ramillies* was bought as she is on the seabed by Mike Borrow, who is now one of the leading figures in the research of the deep, deep ocean, and David Langfield.

But when I look down on Ramillies Cove my concern is not with such things. I can only think of William Wise, ordinary seamen, who was last ashore from the stern of the vessel. He jumped and the ship fell upon him. His leg was smashed. And, as with fear written on his face, he looked back, there was no ship there. In other words, he dragged himself up the rocks with a trailing, useless leg – in that short time 600 men had died and *H.M.S. Ramillies* had ceased to exist.

The last word on any wreck belongs to the divers who go down to her where she lies. There was, of course, a great deal of salvage done on the *Ramillies.* Bob Page of Kingsbridge Watersports, who has dived on the site very recently, has only ever seen two cannon left there. There is a third but you'll find that on top of the Shippen Rock in Hope Cove. The idea was to have a memorial and a flagstaff but for some reason it did not happen. The majority of the remains in Ramillies Cove lie in one gully. There, together, are cannon balls, musket shot and lead sheeting.

Before me as I write is a cannonball, which was dug up together with others from the garden of 'Woodbine' by my grandfather in the 1920's. As I remember it – and I was small at the time – there were three kinds of cannonball, one of each, in the glassed-in porch at the front of the house. There was a massive one which I couldn't lift, a slightly smaller one, and the very much smaller one which I have now,

They were rusty but not in bad condition. How did they come to be under the earth of that garden from which the nearest open sea is about a mile away? There were two stories. One was that they had been fired from Spanish Armada ships. Small as I was, it struck me as remarkable that all three should have arrived at the same point almost simultaneously.

The second story was that these were the ammunition for a

Civil War battery which had been there to defend Thurlestone for the King and against Cromwell. Well, I suppose such a battery could only have three shot left of different sizes, but there is no record of such armaments – the nearest battle being that for Salcombe Castle.

It wasn't until I was writing this book that the probable explanation of those cannonballs occurred to me. Surely they must come from *Ramillies*? We know a great deal of salvage went on. We know too the souvenirs are often soon discarded. That would explain the varying sizes.

H.M.S. Ramillies had on board thirty-two-pounders, eighteen-pounders, twelve-pounders, and six-pounders. I think, allowing for a child's magnification of the size of anything, that those cannonballs of my grandfather's were eighteen, twelve and six-pounders from the wreck of that ship. Certainly the one I have weighs nearly five-pounds and might well have lost the missing ounces by scaling, after immersion in sea-water and then neglect by burial.

12. Watch the Wall, My Darling ...

So there was looting. Which local people regarded as their right – a right to anything which would raise their pitifully low standard of living.

And there was wrecking. Which meant luring a ship ashore. And no one would admit to that. And there was smuggling. Which meant brandy for the parson, 'baccy for the clerk, and money for everyone.

Very few people in the West Country denounced smuggling or failed to take part in it. In fact, the West Country was where you found the real smuggling experts. It is accepted as fact that more rum and brandy were smuggled into Devon and Cornwall in the 1700's than came legally into the Port of London.

General statistics about smuggling are easy to obtain. It is when you try to narrow the action down to Thurlestone and district that the sources fine down to a very few which are actually documented.

There are plenty of blanket statements such as this one: 'The coast extending from Bolt Tail by Hope Cove and around Bolberry Down and Soar Mill Cove [Soar, by the way, is pronounced 'sewer' locally] was notorious for smuggling . . . it was common in those days for farmers, on taking out their horses to work in the fields in the morning, to find them in a state of inexplicable exhaustion. . . .'

Well, it sounds good stuff, but honestly I doubt it. If you think carefully about it, the last place you are going to anchor for long enough to unload your illicit cargo is in front of an inhospitable coastline like that. Of course, the odd barrel of brandy and rum may have come ashore that way, but for big time operations I think you can rule such a place out of any smuggler's calculations.

Imagine being caught in the dark with a sudden squall from the South or South-West. Your smuggling career would be very short indeed. No, for decent smuggling you needed Bigbury Bay.

You needed quiet inlets like Newton Ferrers. Or the entrance to the Erme. Or Burgh Island. Or Bantham and the Avon. Or Yarmer Sands, or Thurlestone Sands or Hope Cove. What you did not need were dangerous onshore rocks and precipitous cliffs.

It is important to realise that smuggling ships were still sailing ships, not tank landing craft that could run up the beach and send their cargo hurtling ashore in Land-Rovers. Everything had to be ferried ashore from a sailing ship in small boats. And that took time.

No I prefer to go back to documented sources. And so I come again to the little book of the Reverend Frank Egerton Coope, called *Thurlestone Church and Parish.* In his book, Mr Coope pays tribute to one of his predecessors, the Rev P. A. Ilbert, who intended to set down all he could find out about the history of Thurlestone.

Unfortunately, the Rev P. A. Ilbert died before he could publish what he had found, but Mr Coope took up the task. His reason for doing so was simple. He wrote in his preface: 'Owing to the advent of the railway the old state of things is rapidly passing away. The old people who remembered the smuggling days and who firmly believed in witchcraft, have, during the twenty and more years I have been here, been nearly all gathered to their fathers . . . The next rector who comes here will find a different world from that in which we so recently found ourselves. The old state of things can never exist again, and therefore it ought to be recorded.'

The railway has, of course, come and gone, thanks to the Beeching axe. But Coope summed up neatly the reason for nearly every factual book: 'the old state of things can never exist again, and therefore it ought to be recorded'. As far as the history of Thurlestone is concerned, the present day is in his debt. And as far as facts about smuggling are concerned, we are all in his debt also.

He managed to extract from Sir Courtenay Ilbert, the eldest son of the Rev P. A. Ilbert, a foreword. And that foreword lifts the lid on some of the smuggling in the area: 'One evening,' wrote Sir Courtenay, 'my father went down to Buckland to visit a dying parishioner, one of the last survivors of an earlier, and maybe more lawless, generation. It was a wild and stormy night, and the wind howling outside recalled old memories. "Lord, sir," were almost his last words, "Lord, sir, what a night for a wrack!" '

That one sentence, in my opinion, tells more about those vanished times than anything else I have read. But Sir Courtenay was not finished. He continued: 'Soon after the middle of the last century my father had a visit from a cousin of his, a retired admiral, who lived at Plymouth. The two sat together on the Rectory lawn and I listened to their talk.

' "The first important job that I had," said the admiral, "was to intercept a cargo of spirits which, we were told, was to be landed somewhere on the Thurlestone coast. I was only a middy, and I was very proud of my job. I picked my men and brought them over from Plymouth, whether by sea or not I forget, but anyhow I got them here.

' "When the evening came I posted them under the cliffs on Yarmouth sands, where we heard the landing was to take place. We waited and waited until I got impatient, especially as I thought I heard the sound of oars. So I ventured stealthily out from the cliff towards the sea. Yes, it certainly was the plash of oars, and very near too.

' "I took hold of my whistle to summon my men, but, before it reached my lips, it was snatched from my hand, a gag was stuffed in my mouth, my arms and legs were tightly pinioned, and I found myself standing, like a helpless idiot, whilst half a dozen strapping girls danced round me.

' "And there I had to stand, whilst the kegs were leaded and carried off inland. Perhaps to your church porch, Mr Rector, but all this was long before your time. Then and not till then, was I released. It was a cloudy night, but the moon shone out at intervals and by its light I was able to mark the faces of those girls."

'As the Admiral talked he cast inquisitive glances at an old woman who was hobbling about on the lawn. She was a neighbour of ours who lived in a cottage just across the road, and who used occasionally to take her pleasure in the Rectory grounds.

' "Yes," went on the Admiral, "I marked very carefully the faces of those girls. And she," he said, pointing with his finger, "and she was one of them." I wonder whether she was. When I knew her she was an irreproachable old lady to whom we were much attached.'

Was she? We shall never know. But it does make you wonder about the charming ladies who decorate Thurlestone's streets today! Are they the daughters of what amounted to a female smuggling ring based on Thurlestone?

Both women and men smugglers had an easy time until the proper policing of the coast in the 1830's, when a better coastguard system was introduced. But more coastguards, better paid and trained, did not stop the smuggling.

Far from it. One Thurlestone man who died in 1900 at the age of ninety-one told his Rector: 'Many and many a time I carried up a ladder as many as fifty barrels of spirits on a dark night, and hid them on the top of the roof of the church porch behind the battlements. Us always kept the tower door locked them times, lest one should go up and look down over.'

The Thurlestone parson benefited exactly as in the words of Kipling's poem: 'Five and twenty ponies, trotting through the dark, brandy for the Parson, 'baccy for the Clerk. Them as asks no questions isn't told a lie. Watch the wall, my darling, while the Gentlemen go by!'

Well, the Thurlestone parson did benefit until the coming in 1839 of Peregrine Arthur Ilbert – and Peregrine Arthur 'indignantly refused to accept it'.

A smuggling run would need a considerable time to complete. And though, of course, I was never an eye-witness to such a run in Thurlestone, I was able to watch one in Spain just after the Second World War. The town concerned emptied – not suddenly, but it is true to say that all of a sudden I was aware that there was no one round. Civil police were conspicuous by their absence and, as for the Guardia, they, too, seemed to have a sudden need to do something important elsewhere.

It didn't take me long to find the town's population – at a cove just outside the town they were all busily engaged in heaving, not spirits (they were too cheap in Spain to bother about), but English and American cigarettes in vast quantities up from the beach. It didn't seem like something illegal. Everyone was so cheerful and helpful that they might well have been bringing in some cargo donated by Lease-Lend to help an under-privileged community.

All the bars in town had the cigarettes almost openly on sale the next day – and life resumed as though such a landing had never happened.

This was what impressed me most about the whole operation. That it had been organised down to the tiniest degree. That there was no sense of guilt. That the ship in the bay was there for some considerable time while cargo was unloaded. And that, as suddenly as she had come, she was gone and life reverted to normal as though nothing unusual had happened.

This, I am sure, is what happened with smuggling in the South Hams. There was unlikely to be any sense of guilt, but a smuggling run did take some considerable part of the night, or day. Of course, it was not always possible to land the kegs and get them up to the village to a reasonable hiding place. In such cases the kegs did not actually come ashore that day or night at all, but were dumped in the sea between the shore and the rocks, from which Thurlestone Rock rears up as a perfect sighting mark for the kegs' subsequent recovery. Smugglers called this 'sowing the crop' and it was done remarkably quickly so the smuggling boat was in and out without having to stop.

Why use that part of the coast – Thurlestone Sands – instead of, say, Yarmer? The reason, if you walk the ground, is perfectly obvious. If you stand on the edge of the golf course and look down on Yarmer (or Yarmouth, as the Ordnance Survey insists on calling it) you can see right through the gin-clear water. It would have to be a pretty dim Revenue man who could not see the kegs from such a vantage point. And though Yarmer was closest to the village and all sorts of hiding places, Thurlestone Sands cannot be looked down on immediately to the front and does give you several escape routes if the damned Customs officers swooped. You could be away to South Milton, or South Huish, or even Outer Hope, given a fair chance, before they could even sort themselves out in the thick, soft, Devon dark.

Leas Foot was another favoured landing place. The Rev Frank Coope records that a woman called Mrs Hingstone had bought a block of salt from a small-time smuggler there – there was a duty on salt – and dressed the block in baby clothes in case she was stopped.

Mrs Hingstone had acted wisely. She was soon overtaken by a man on a horse who is quaintly described as 'the preventive officer'.* Says he: 'That is a very quiet baby of yours, Mrs Hingstone.' Says she: 'Ees fy; he gives me no trouble at all.' And it seems she got away with it.

Mr Coope is also responsible for reporting that so popular at one time was Leas Foot for this sort of landing that a farmer had to drive his sheep back and forth across the sand to wipe out the traces of the smugglers.

One of the favourite hiding places for smuggled goods in Cornwall were the shafts of the tin mines. In Devon the most favoured places were thatched roofs. Quite recently when a thatched cottage was being demolished – and it is impossible to understand what sort of mind would do such a thing anyway – the ceiling collapsed under the blows of destruction. And down from the ceiling with the rubble and out of the thatch came what was obviously a smuggler's horde.

Coins of all kinds, together with a long-forgotten keg or two, came tumbling down. And the interesting thing about the horde was that the coins were all of foreign manufacture and all around the 1800 vintage. My interest quickened when I heard about that, because I have read that some old title deeds of the area around Thurlestone seem to indicate that the Portuguese moidore was once legal enough tender in Thurlestone to be accepted as part of the purchase price. (The moidore, literally gold money, was a gold coin worth about the same as a gold sovereign in the times in which it was used as common currency.)

If you look at the map or, better still, look at the Avon at Bantham, you will not have the slightest doubt that this is good smuggling country. Two men seem to have shared the major part of the trade. Tom Crocker, or Croker, worked out of Bigbury and Nat Cleverly captained a boat out of Bantham.

There can be no argument that Bantham was a smuggling

*In 1822 there were three lines of defence against the smugglers. One: The Revenue cutters, which boarded boats at sea looking for contraband; two, the preventive boats which searched the coastal waters and inshore creeks; and thirdly, the Riding Officers, who were mounted and armed to deal with 'runs' on land. It was presumably one of these mounted men who intercepted Mrs Hingstone.

centre. Kegs were landed there and brought up the hill from the quay in carts covered over with seaweed – ostensibly for use as manure. (It is interesting to note that seaweed manure is superb for asparagus and the rich red soil of Devon is the ideal bed for this delicious vegetable. As asparagus is a native British plant and has been grown here for centuries, it could be that the seaweed was normally brought up from the shore for inland beds of asparagus.)

The kegs were sometimes hidden, according to the Rev Frank Coope, in Whiddon's blacksmith's shop – a house now known as 'Whiddon's' stands on the site today. A smoke-grimed trap-door led to the loft over the two forges, but owing to the grime which covered them afresh each day, the existence of the trap-door could not be seen from below and once the kegs of brandy were up, they were safe for a while.

In fact, we are wrong to talk about kegs in a smuggling context. In Thurlestone and district they were known as 'tubs' or 'half-ankers'. An anker held about eight gallons.

David Phillipson, in his excellent book on smuggling* – he was in H.M. Customs himself for fifteen years so should know what he is talking about – says that during his service he was able to look through records of the eighteenth century and these records smashed any ideas he might have had about smuggling in those days being a romantic Robin Hood-type occupation (he quotes the severing of the two hands of a Customs officer with a cutlass blade as he was about to board a suspect vessel as one horrible example).

But he does note also: 'Further research has strengthened my conviction that smugglers (with honorable exceptions, notably among Westcountrymen) were as ripe a bunch of villainous, bloodthirsty and contemptible cut-throats as ever besmirched England's fair name.'

The ghosts of those smugglers, who, after you have had a good meal at the Sloop at Bantham, crowd in from the dark outside the narrow high-banked lanes, must thank Mr Phillipson for excluding them from his strictures. I must say that in my research I have found little evidence of violence in the Thurlestone district during the numerous smuggling runs – most of this

**Smuggling, a history 1700-1970* by David Phillipson, published by David and Charles Ltd.

area of Devon smugglers seem to have gone exceptionally quietly when caught by the Revenue men.

Not that they had not a great deal of money at stake. In the 1750's a tub of brandy cost a little over 16s in France or the Channel Islands. The duty on a tub worked out at about 32s, but a smuggled tub went for 25s, no questions asked. So you have some idea of the profit on a heavy run.

Mind you, it wasn't all profit – some of it was damned hard work. The Bantham boat of Cleverly would work the Channel Islands where there was then no duty at all, or later the port of Roscoff in France. And there was no easing up when the Channel gales heralded the start of winter. Smuggling was a full-time occupation and went on all year round.

The weather took its toll, of course, and one of the most extraordinary smuggling casualty stories is that of Philip Kingcup's boat which drifted ashore near Hope with all tubs slung along the side ready to be dropped (in Thurlestone?) – and not a soul aboard.

The story is best told in the words of a fellow smuggler, quoted apparently verbatim by Lieutenant The Honorable H. N. Shore, who was a coastguard officer of the Royal Navy at Fowey in 1870, and later became Lord Teignmouth.

The smuggler is identified only by the initials 'R.H.' and those are obviously not his true initials at all.* Even so, the quotation has the ring of truth. It goes like this: 'That's true what you say about poor Phil Kingcup being lost. I was coming back from Cherbourg the same night; werry stormy, it was, though I've seen it wuss, still there was the douce of a kick-up of sea.

'We was going to start together; but when we got under weigh Phil sung out they wouldn't be ready for another half-hour – had to get their to'sl down and stowed. However, after a bit, we see'd 'em following, and that was the last was ever seen of the boat under sail.

'Next that was heard of her was when she drifted on shore,

*This quote appears in Henry Shore's booklet *Old Foye Days* (Part II) published in 1907 (reprinted by Frank Graham in 1966). It is sub-titled 'An Authentic Account of the Exploits of the Smugglers in and around the Port of Fowey'. This book and *Smuggling Days and Ways* by the same author, published in 1892, (reprinted by E. P. Publishing Ltd in 1972) are two of the few accounts of smuggling by someone who was actually taking part – in Shore's case, of course, trying to stop smuggling.

with all her tubs hung round her, and the ballast gone, by Hope Cove. The bodies – four of 'em – was seen lying on the bottom, in deep water, just outside. I saw them mysel; t'was the strangest sight I ever see'd, for you could tell their faces as they laid on the bottom, it was that clear.'

Knowing that the Reverend Peregrine Ilbert had refused to accept a present of spirits from the smugglers of Thurlestone makes this quote from another smuggler, identified only as 'J.H.' even more amusing:

'The passons was werry different back-along to what they is now; reckon they knew the wally o' pure sperrits, and warn't too grand to buy them from the pooe chaps what risked their lives to keep the parish supplied. 'Twas soverin' remedy in collic and brown typhus, when doctors warn't so common in the land, and med'cins was dear for poor folk. . . .

'Lord, what a pretty lot of tubs I've see'd passed into church of a Saturday night! I don't 'spose there's a church anywhere nigh the shore but what's had a crop of goods laid in it. The passons didn't mind – of course they was paid their tithes all fair and above board. Aye, and there's been some fine sarmons preached over the goods on a Sunday morning, seeing as how there was allus a grand muster of church folk marnin' arter a run.'

In the case of Thurlestone Church, of course, the sermons were preached under the goods as the tubs of brandy were all up on the roof of the church porch.

'J.H.' has one other lovely story to tell: 'A passon up Padstow way, time wrecking was allowed back-along. Well, one Sunday morning – leastways that's what old dad used to say, a ship got on to the Gull Rock while the folk was at church, and old Ephraim Blowey – that was the sexton, having been bred to the sea, always kept his weather eye liftin' seawards, and twigged it in a moment, and shouts "Wreck!" and the congregation was on their feet in a jiffy. But the passon, being a conscientious man and werry strict about doing things right and proper, was all for fairplay –

'Stop! stop!' cried he, 'at least one prayer,
'Let me get down, and all start fair.'

It would be wrong, however, to lead you into thinking that Thurlestone, Bantham and Salcombe were the hot-bed for the country's smuggling. The truth is that there were very few parts of the coastal areas of the whole country – and that includes Scotland, Ireland and Wales – which were not used for smuggling. And very few people from the lowest to the highest were prepared to turn down a drop of the hard stuff at a soft price.

The parson would preach against it from his pulpit and then ask no questions about the keg that appeared at the back door of the parsonage as a gift for him. The lords and squires often had a good snigger over a glass of fine brandy at the dinner table, winking in exaggerated fashion about a fine new wine merchant that they had found almost on their own doorstep. And the village labourer probably had the best excuse of all for taking part – at times he could not earn enough to buy bread for his family from honest labour. So who can blame him for carrying a keg or two for good pay up from the sea shore?

Things had reached a fine state indeed when in a debate on the Smuggling Bill of 1736 it was said that: 'In some parts of the maritime counties the whole people are so generally engaged in smuggling that it is impossible to find a jury that will, upon trial, do justice to an officer of the revenue in any case whatever.

'In those counties where smuggling is become general, the majority of the coroner's inquests always consists of smugglers so that it has been found by experience that these inquests always bring the officer and his assistants in guilty of murder, even though it be made clearly appear, by the most undoubted testimonies, that the killing happened *de defendendo*.'

Something had to be done – the boats from Bantham, Salcombe, the Yealm and Plymouth were calling so regularly at Guernsey for cargos of spirits and tobacco, salt, silks, brocades, that they could almost have published a time-table. In 1767 Guernsey and Jersey were taken out of the smuggler's top ten ports of call by the establishment of Customs.

As a result, the illicit trade simply moved its activities to Roscoff on Cap Finistére. The French were delighted and in 1769 made it a free port. A little port used only by a few fishermen, Roscoff was suddenly a place of great importance. True, it had had its moments before that – Mary, Queen of Scots had landed there in 1548 on her way to marry the

Dauphin, and Bonnie Prince Charlie came back to France through the port after his defeat at Culloden.

So the South Devon boats now took on their cargoes at Roscoff, and, though it sounds fantastic, English, Scots, Irish and Guernsey merchants set up establishments there to supply them! Business boomed. In twelve days in March, 1833, nine West Country boats left Roscoff with 850 tubs on board. At about four gallons a tub, that's a mighty lot of booze.

Roscoff, of course, had its heyday and as the Government finally clamped down on smuggling by establishing the Coastguard service and cutting down on Customs duties, so it sank back to being the pleasant port it is today. Today its fame is based not on smuggling, but on onions, for it is from Roscoff that the French onion-sellers invade Britain.

The smuggling 'runs' carried out in Thurlestone cannot have been small. Remember the old man who said he could recall carrying fifty barrels of spirits up to the roof of the Church porch in one night, and that he had done this 'many and many a time'? That works out at some 200 gallons a time – and we don't know that all the 'run' was hidden in the Church.

Having researched the anatomy of a smuggling operation, it is interesting to apply what I found out to the Thurlestone area:

Somebody must have been the principal – the man who put up the money to buy the goods in Roscoff. Or maybe it was a group of Devon worthies. The landing spot was chosen – Yarmer Sands. There was, of course, no golf course there then, just gorse bushes and tufty, hummocky ground. The time was fixed and the word put round. Heaving, say, a hundred barrels ashore quickly needs organisation and, most important of all, manpower. So the day before the run the word would be out in Thurlestone, Bantham, Buckland, Milton and South Huish that there was five shillings per man available for a night's work.

A rendezvous was chosen and at the appointed hour, the tub-carriers would assemble in the darkness and remain quiet. The Revenue men would be alert for any noise or any light. The time chosen for a 'run' was usually early in the night. Early darkness was not so quiet a time as the midnight hours and no one wanted a large number of men – fifty would be needed for our hundred tubs – hanging about near a beach. The longer they had to wait the more likely they would be to become noisy.

A slight plash of oars, a crunch in the darkness and a boat touches the beach. Down come the tub-carriers in a mob. They make a noise – no talking but still a noise – but it is speed which matters now. The tubs are already slung together in two's. Over the tub-carriers' heads go the ropes and, like back-and-front St Bernards, they stumble off into the night. The load is heavy but a boat can be cleared in three minutes, five at the most, and then all that remains of the 'run' is the trodden path down the beach. That is, unless someone kindly drives his sheep flock over the marks in the dawn light.

The tub-carriers split up now. One lot heads for the Church – there are no roads and expensive houses in their way as they would find now, just rough ground, spinneys, bramble patches and the fear of the Revenue man who may be lurking somewhere in the dark ahead.

But he isn't there and the casks are safely stowed in their hiding place in the church. The men are paid and given a generous jug of brandy for themselves. Some come up the village street, past my cottage, heading for their homes.

Out in the dark somewhere else another fifty casks are heading for, or have reached, a different hiding place – for the smuggler was a great believer in that old saying about not putting all your tubs in one hideyhole. I don't know where that other hidey-hole was. Somewhere in Bantham or Buckland? Unlikely. If Bantham was the target they would have planned the 'run,' nearer to home. It can't have been too far from the landing place – those tubs were darned heavy.

But as the Coastguards got better organised it was not always common-sense to land the tubs on the beach. Then the ship carrying the tubs would come in as close as she dared in the dusk – take her bearings on some prominent landmark and as she turned out to sea, cut away the lashings which held the tubs along the ship's side. Suitably weighted, they would sink to the bottom – or nearly to the bottom – and an anchor system would hold them in place.

It was now up to the locals to gather in 'the crop'. Hope Cove was a centre of this activity. The crabbing work normally carried out from there was a fine excuse to be hauling up lines to objects on the bottom and our 'crop-sowing' smuggler made sure that he sowed in places where the crabbers could legitimately be at work. They would know the marks and would grapple for the tubs and linking lines during their normal hauling of their crab pots. Of course, sometimes 'crops' were lost and never found, but it is some indication of the amount of money to be made by smuggling that if one cargo out of three was successfully landed, the business paid. And paid well.

It is interesting to note that in all local stories about the 'preventive officers' which have survived, it is the officer who seems a fool and the local men whose cunning defeats the uniformed simpletons. A classic example is that of the two Thurlestone men at an undated time who were carrying smuggled tubs across Aveton Gifford bridge (pronounced 'Awton Jifford') when they saw the preventive man coming from the other side. So they lowered the kegs over the side of the bridge on the ropes by which they had them slung over their shoulders, sat on the ropes and enjoyed the scenery until the officer had gone by. It is a good story and Thurlestone men today are undoubtedly good at coping with the various demands tourism pushes upon them, but it does sound too good to be true.

I am, however, more inclined to believe the story of Sir Courtenay Ilbert as quoted by the Rev. Frank Coope. 'When I was a boy,' said Sir Courtenay – and this would place it sometime in the 1870's – a schooner ran aground at the river end of Bantham sands. She was laden with French wine and Mr Gladstone had not yet lowered the duties on claret. We boys went down to see the fun.

'When we got there we found a great assembly of villagers on the sands. The barrels had been brought ashore. The coastguard men were in charge of them, and the senior coastguard was giving directions. "We'm bound to stave they casks in," he said. "And," he added after a pause, "I'm thinking that over there would be the proper place for to stave 'em in". He pointed to the further end of the bay, where at low tide, there are several nice clean rock basins full of salt water. There may have been an imperceptible wink, but, in any case, the crowd were off in a trice to the village, whilst the coastguards began to trundle the barrels solemnly across the sands.

'Before they reached their destination the villagers returned with mops and swabs and receptables of every kind, cans, jugs and the like. The pools were carefully emptied and cleaned and the barrels were so placed that when they were staved in, the contents flowed into the rock basins, whence they were in due course decanted. For a considerable time the parish swam with claret.'

Judging by this and the local smuggling activities, Thurlestone, Bantham and the like sound as though they had little cause to fear the rare cold snaps of winter in this part of Devon. And if the rolling English drunkard really did make the rolling English road, then there is a simple explanation of the winding lanes around my cottage – they are all obviously the result of too much cider, claret and brandy!

13. *All a Question of Time*

Immediately after *Just-a-Cottage* was published in 1974 I knew there would have to be another edition. So many people wrote to me, rang me, stopped me in the village street - all with precious pieces of information - that I knew I wouldn't be happy until I had a chance to expand the original book.

Fortunately I have been spared the task of starting all over again because my new publisher decided, that he would like to reprint the earlier version and then add some of the new material I had collected. So that is what we have done.

What has happened to the village since I first wrote this book?

Sadly, Peter Grose of the Thurlestone Hotel is with us no more.

He did so much for the village that it is not surprising that his funeral was so hugely attended that the Church could not contain all who wished to pay their last respects. Two of his sons, David and Graham carry on the tradition and the hotel.

Another loss is Arthur Stidston. Jim Elliott of Bantham too is dead and habourmaster in his place is Hugh Cater, who builds yawls the way they did long years ago. Well, almost the way they did. Hugh's seem to go faster.

Dennis Cresdee is no longer master of the Sloop at Bantham. He has moved and the delightful old inn is now in the capable hands of Neil Girling and his wife Gail.

The Shermans are no longer at the Village Stores in Thurlestone. He and his wife have moved away and their place has been taken by the energetic Bob and Kay Morley. And Kay's Scots accent mixes delightfully with the Devon burrs.

Broads Dairy, which has the Post Office under its wing, has not changed hands. Mrs. Mary Bromfield copes with the summer rush with endless patience, but her two sons, Gordon and Peter, who run the farm, suffered a major set-back on January 31st, 1979 when a great fire ravaged the old buildings.

They are now rebuilt.

Having brought village matters up to date, I can only say to those who have said to me: 'Why didn't you ask me?', 'I didn't know you knew'. To those who said: 'Why didn't you use what I told you?', I can only say: 'There is such a thing as libel m'dear!' Time always proves you wrong. In my ignorance in the first edition I was foolish enough to say that the earliest map of Thurlestone with any detail on it was the Tithe Map of 1840. I was wrong. How wrong I only knew when, after guidance, I went to the Devon Record Office in Exeter. There I was shown not only the Courtenay Map of 1777, but the detailed survey with it of Sir William Courtenay's agent, George Lang.

George Lang had done a good job for his master, Sir William Courtenay, who was born in 1742, succeeded to the baronetcy as Earl of Devon when he was 20 and died in Grosvenor Square, London, in 1788.

The map was interesting (see plan, page 139). The survey book was fascinating.

The map dances with names that are old England. Opposite my cottage on the right-hand side of the Bantham road are fields called the North Stroll, Higher Desolate, Lower Desolate, Higher Pipers Bench, and on the left-hand side of the road heading to Bantham surrounding Rockhill, are Forty Acres (and with English logic being nothing like it) further on Balls Park and Hill Park.

And racing down the road to the sea, the village stops at the Church and finally a footpath weaves its way to Leys Foot Sands. (Stand up those who said I was wrong to call it *Leas* Foot!)

But the important thing was that there on the 1777 map is my cottage bold and clear with the passageway emerging at the back onto a path which goes down the centre of the land belonging to the cottage. Land which as it now contains the Frosts' swimming pool in the garden of their Home Cottage, should give me the moral right to use the pool at all times!

The survey book of George Lang in beautifully curly writing gave me other delights. My little cottage had another name - 'Lakeman's Cottage' and the owner was Walter Steer. True, it shared the name of 'Lakeman's Cottage' with Len Jeffery's cottage next door which is clearly marked as being '2 dwellings with outhouses' and the 1777 owner, Hugh Hardy.

The map and survey book provide some surprises. My earlier researches had led me to believe that Home Cottage, next door to me, had once been three cottages. The 1777 survey shows that was once five dwellings. Right next door to Just-a-Cottage was Joan Lidstone's Cottage, which was divided into three dwellings, and next to that up the hill was Cradles Cottage, which was divided into two.

My research continues, but in the village lives a man whose diligent work makes my efforts look very small. Dr. Neville C. Oswald, F.R.C.P. of the Old Rectory, has done an enormous amount of research into the parish registers and the baptism and burial records and his work on 'Thurlestone Families' and a larger paper on epidemics in the South Hams have been published by the Devon Association.

Anyone who is interested in Thurlestone will find the extract from his 'Thurlestone Families' paper, which forms the appendix totally absorbing.

Most of the rest of this chapter, and all of the next, are made up of the memories of others who knew the village well in days gone by.

I received many letters full of memories. All looked back at Thurlestone through a golden haze. In those letters the sun always shone and a drowsy heat, through which Red Admiral butterflies fluttered effortlessly around the village, seemed to be uppermost in the minds of the writers.

Only one person who wrote to me included a storm in his memories. This was Geoffrey Inchbald, author and historian, who is now 85. He too told me I was welcome to use any of his memories of Thurlestone.

It was Mr. Inchbald's father who built The Grey House (now 'The Downs') and it took three years to complete. The Plymouth stone was brought round by sea, dumped on the nearest beach and then carried by cart up to the site on the high ground above the village.

The house was completed in late August 1909 and the family had only just moved in when the storm, which was rated as a hurricane, struck. Writes Mr. Inchbald: 'After an uneasy and anxious night, we awoke early and gazed out on an astonishing scene. There seemed to be a giant snowstorm in progress but

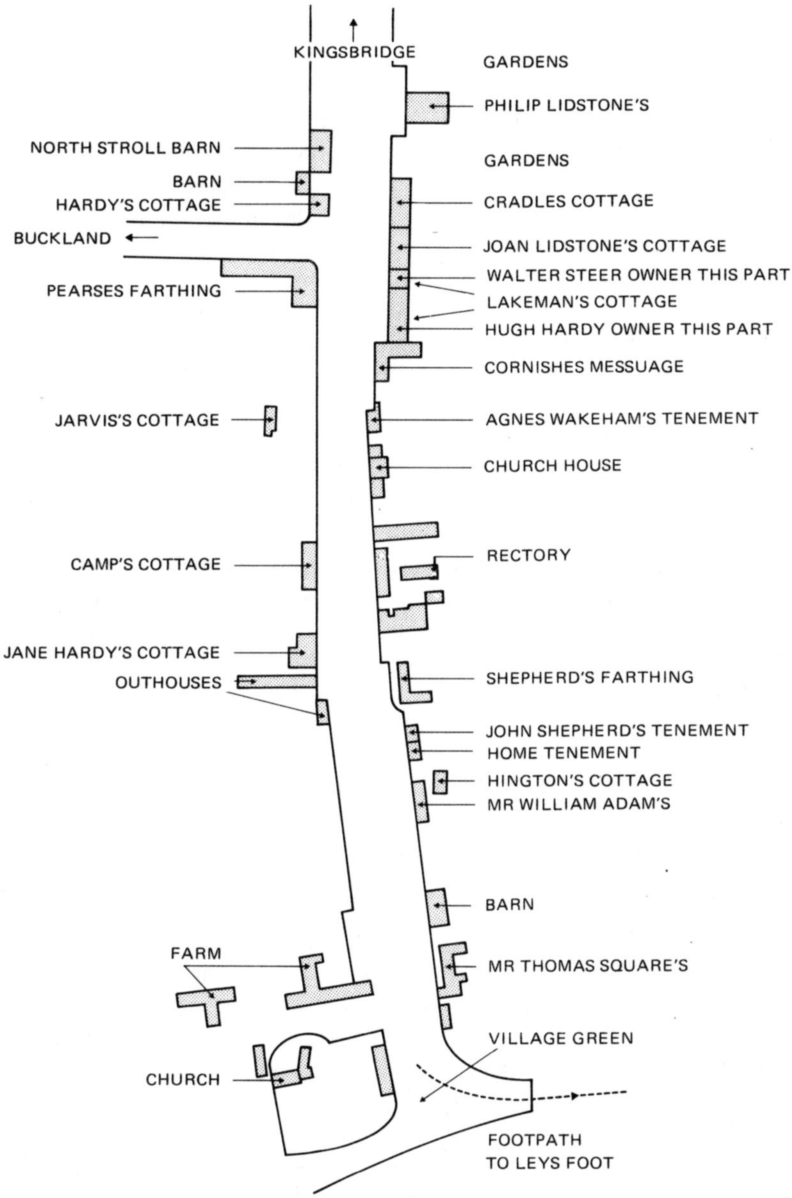

Thurlestone Village in 1777

with some of the flakes as big as footballls and of a dirty yellowish colour. For a moment it was difficult to grasp that what we were looking at was not snow but spume driven off the tops of the waves by winds in excess of 100 m.p.h., flung over the cliffs, and hurled inland at a height of anything up to 500 feet. All this accompanied by such a pandemonium of noise that you could hardly hear yourself speak and also by a real anxiety on the part of the older members of the family as to whether a brand new house could stand up indefinitely to such a battering. But it had been built well and they need not have feared. There was only one real incident. We were playing in the attic at the top of the house, which we used as a games room, when there was a crash and a slate came through the window narrowly missing one of my brothers in the process. Within seconds the wind had got underneath that particular section of the roof, which literally disintegrated though fortunately the hundreds of slates of which it consisted were instantly carried away and no more came through the window.

But the damage was confined to that section and, so far as I can remember, the rest of the roof remained intact. In the evening some of us emerged from the house and fought our way to the cliffs and down to the beach where the foam was lying several feet high and continually being replenished as great chunks were torn away and flung over the cliffs. Going home was even more difficult on account of the fact that, when you were forced into a run by that irresistible pressure from behind, it was almost impossible to stop and we certainly established a two-way record on that memorable day, which was described as the worst storm within living memory.

'After my mother's death in 1925 the house was sold and became Downs Hotel. Some years ago it was gutted by fire which was shown on television, but it has since been rebuilt.'

Mr. Inchbald, knew the Rector's family, the Coopes, well. And their daughters - 'with one or two or more of whom my brothers and myself were continuously and successively falling in love over quite a long period ot years'.

He remembers my grandfather and his Jack the Ripper stories well too: 'There was an old man in the village who had spent his working life as a member of the Metropolitan Police Force in London. When the First War broke out all the coastguards, being either R.N.R. or R.N.V.R., were promptly recalled to the Navy so that the coast which had hitherto been patrolled both day and night was left completely unguarded at a time when it most needed protection. Volunteers were called for and our little community was allotted the stretch of coast from Thurlestone to Bantham.

My brother Jack and I were only too pleased to give our services during the month of August, after which we were both due at camp on Salisbury Plain from where he went direct into the Army with a commission in the Devonshire Regiment and I returned to Winchester for two more terms.

We patrolled in couples, and he and I always selected the period from 2 a.m. to 7 a.m. as distinct from 9 p.m. to 2 a.m. as this gave us the opportunity for an hour's shooting in the early morning before we returned home for breakfast with several rabbits slung round our middles in addition, if we were lucky, to one or two ducks. We were on duty most nights and we had to make contact with the earlier patrol at a particular bunker on the golf course, where we used to have a little gossip and refreshment before taking over. On several occasions we met up in this way with our ex-policeman friend and used to listen avidly to his tales of crime in London, and very murky crime at that, including grisly details of the exploits and methods of Jack the Ripper.

In later years, I remember, a little ritual used to observed on Sunday mornings by the ex-policeman. This had nothing to do with the Sabbath as such but on my way back from church I had to pass the entrance way to his house, which was near the top of the village street, and even if I was not alone he used to indicate by a variety of winks and gestures that I was to shake off my companions and slip through a little gate which led to his back garden in which there was a small cottage. There he would be waiting for me with a twinkle in his eye and a finger on his lips to indicate that complete quiet must be observed so as not to attract the attention of his wife who was cooking the Sunday dinner in the house.

Inside the cottage which was almost pitch dark, he would go into a corner and conjure up a pint or so of the strongest, alcoholic beverage which it has ever been my fortune, or misfortune, to consume. The real top class 100% draught

Devonshire cider which those casks used to contain bore about as much resemblance to the ordinary bottled cider as a slug of neat whisky to a glass of milk, after a couple of tumblerfuls it was a much as I could do to stand up let alone to see straight. It was very livery stuff, and I would have preferred beer, but how I used to enjoy those Sunday sessions! In fact I became quite a regular church-goer!'

So it seems that my grandfather will be remembered not for the length of his service with the London police, but for the strength of his cider in Devon. Perhaps he would have liked it that way!

One other letter among the many which came out of the blue proved the key to some remarkable memories.

It was signed Monica Winkle. Mrs. Winkle turned out to be the former Monica Coope, one of those daughters of the Reverend Frank Egerton Coope, Rector of Thurlestone from 1897 to 1912, who so fascinated the Inchbald brothers.

We met and enjoyed a lunch over which the Thurlestone scandal flowed thick and fast. They say that the air of Thurlestone makes old ladies young. As proof you only had to see Monica! She had written her memoirs and she gave them to me. I have only been able to include part of them here, but in time I hope to print them all in full. Certainly, as you will see, Monica Coope was a natural writer with a gift of evoking the past. Sadly she died a year ago. This is her story.

14. *Monica's Memoirs*

by MONICA WINKLE

When I close my eyes to look at Thurlestone I see nothing that is new or recent, but it is just as it was in our childhood days. I am at the top of the village, looking down the hill, with Mrs. Pound's sweet shop on my left, the tiny post office on Buckland Corner, and the cottages, white-washed and thatched, with bee-hive windows, elbowing each other down the hill until the pink cob wall of the Rectory garden at the bottom stretches into the near distance, framed by the high elms through which one can glimpse the square beacon tower of Thurlestone Church.

There is much to tell of those days, when nothing seemed to happen except life and death; everyone in our little orbit was of importance to us and their joys and sorrows were ours too. Besides ourselves, only the Ilbert's, the Chandos-Poles, and the Grose's were permanent residents in the village itself, so the influence of the cottage folk was a powerful one, and our contact with them was that of intimate respect.

'They must live in the country, by the sea, in a large house with a big garden. They must learn to be content with simple pleasures that money cannot buy, and every penny we can scrape together must be spent on their education and training.'

Thus spake father, and mother agreed, so we came to Thurlestone, six children and promise of more. It was a far cry from Sussex to Devonshire, and a very weary little band of hope that finally arrived on that winter's evening in 1897, the winter after the great blizzard that had enveloped the Devon moors and valleys, isolated farms and cottages for weeks, and devastated the flocks and herds, starved and buried in the man-high snow-drifts.

The Rectory was an ideal home for us, but not for our mother, who had to adapt herself to oil lamps and candlelight, pumped water, no bathroom, an outside earth closet, rambling passages, vast attics, and not a single cupboard anywhere except a small black hole under the stairs. Apart from the post office and Mrs. Pound's sweet shop, you could not even buy a boot lace without driving into Kingsbridge, nearly five miles away, and although the butcher and baker called at intervals, you had to take what they had brought you, and it was not always good.

'I believe you always send me the old sheep', mother complained to the butcher. 'Well, mum, someone has got to eat them', he answered, civilly enough, and that was that.

Fish? Well, hardly ever. The catches coming in at Hope Cove were already bespoken for the London market, as were the crabs and lobsters scrambling around in the pots in Bigbury Bay.

Later on, as mother got wiser, she sent off a cheque to a Grimsby firm and we got a regular supply once a week, but sometimes it did not travel as quickly as fish should. Of course we had ample milk, eggs, and fresh fruit and vegetables, but even so I marvel now at her ingenuity in producing a good and satisfying meal at least once a day for her large household, consisting as we did of our parents, eleven children, a governess, a nurse, and two maids, not to mention the various daily helps who came in to scrub and launder. Labour was cheap then and there was no lack of helping hands, although there was so much work to do that they often fell by the wayside, and we always seemed to have fresh faces in the kitchen.

We were bonny children, round-faced, blue and hazel-eyed, brown-haired, inheriting our good complexions and clear skins. Mother dressed the older ones in scarlet coats and bonnets, and the comments of the villagers "The little dears, they'm lovely", brought a sharp reproof from our nurse Annie, and the smug look on Mary's face faded!

Katherine, Arthur, Mary, Hilda, Winefride, and Monica. That was the bag so far, but one day a small person toddled up the long passage to mother's room and pummelled on the closed door.

'Who is it?' asked a strange voice.

'It's Baby', I replied.

'No, not Baby any more. Run away my dear, you can't see your mother now.'

A howling despairing form was dragged away by an elder sister, and the twins reigned in my stead.

The nursery was a big sunny room facing over the garden terrace, and communicated with the night nursery. The windows looked out over Bigbury Bay to Bolt Tail, and there also stood Thurlestone Rock, set in the sea like a gigantic pair of trousers, withstanding every storm that buffetted through its high arch, battering at its strong base, and never succeeded in harming it one jot or tittle. At low tide you could clamber out to the Rock and see the lovely cowries walking about the deep pools there. Masses of cowries are washed up every spring and summer on the sands, but the Gulf Stream may be responsible for most of them as other lovely and exotic shells are there in abundance too. Once we hurried down to Lea Foot to see the fleet of "Portugese Men-of-War", and there they were, tiny craft with bright blue sails, being cast ashore in their hundreds, and perishing in the hot sun. I have never seen these queer creatures since then, but they are jelly fish and very poisonous.

There once stood an ancient forest of oak where the sea now takes possession between the Rock and the shore, and one can still pick up fragments of the bog oak in the rock pools at low tide.

Although when we came to Thurlestone there were under four hundred people living there, it was a widely scattered parish, with the hamlets of East and West Buckland, and Bantham, together with outlying farms at Whitley, Aunemouth, and Worthy. Father reckoned to pay a personal visit at every cottage twice during the year, and this entailed visiting at least four afternoons a week all the year round.

He was very particular about this and did not limit himself to the church-going people, as so many lived far off and had duties to their live-stock on Sundays, so they really could not often manage the long walk both ways. Also the chapel folk would always come up to the church for special occasions, and their last journey was to the churchyard overlooking the sea.

In order to spare himself the fatigue of the long hills Dora would be saddled and give Dad a lift when he felt tired. Sometimes one of us would go too, and take turns with father to ride Dora, and look over the top of the high banks. We enjoyed these visits, which were mostly of a social nature, as father never forced religion on people. If an old soul wanted him to say a prayer while he was there he did so, and down I would go on my knobbly knees on the stone floor and join in with a will, and think it very nice. Then up on Dora again and away to the next farm, hoping perhaps for a slice of saffron cake with a blob of cream on top, and a cup of thick, sweet tea.

Mother had no time to go to the far distant cottages, but she was unwearying in little kindnesses in Thurlestone and Buckland, keeping small bundles of cash in her bureau labelled, 'Sick Fund', 'Comforts for Old Folk', with which she supplemented the meagre allowances under parish relief which was then all that was available for those past earning a living; and how their pride suffered in taking it. Being on the parish was only one step above the ignominy of the workhouse.

After the twins were born and came to known as Boydie and Girlie, it became a problem how to transport us all on our daily walks, as it was much too hilly for prams. Then it meant that Brownie the donkey came to live with us, and he had a little saddle with basket panniers each side into which the twins were stowed, while the rest of us took it in turns to perch up on the saddle and rest our legs. We must have made a comic calvalcade, especially when Brownie felt reluctant to proceed and dug his forefeet squarely down, and stayed there. Sometimes the one in the saddle would shoot over his head in the surprise of this sudden halting, but it was not very far to go and he always allowed you to mount again, where you would sit patiently until Brownie decided that it was time to move off again. The twins were sweet little babies, and as toddlers mother dressed them in sailor suits, serge in winter, white drill in summer. They were the pride of her life, and it was a great shock to all of us, (even the deposed ex-baby), when they both fell ill and Boydie died of pneumonia on an Easter Sunday when he was just three years old. I was not yet five, but remember kissing the soft cold baby face, and hearing mother sobbing. I wanted to comfort her and did not know how. There were no more children for two years after that, and then John came, and mother's sad heart bloomed again. There are carved oaken angels flying around the roof of the chancel in Thurlestone Church; they are John's angels, as a thank-you for his birth.

It was a good thing that the Rectory had been built by Mr. Ilbert for his own large family, for it was still big enough to hold us all comfortably. The Ilberts had been there five and fifty years and were part and parcel of the life and existence of Thurlestone.

His widow lived at Rockhill at the top of the village with her daughter Helen and son Donald and his married daughter Mrs. Robert Campbell down at Bantham. The Rectory and Rockhill were both blessed with really beautiful wide staircases coming down into the centre of the hall and giving great character to the houses. Halfway down ours was a long lancet window filled with stained glass, and in the drawing room at Rockhill were two strange circular windows also with stained glass, which entranced us when we were told that they were two of the wheels from the coach which had taken Mr. and Mrs. Ilbert on their honeymoon.

The choir was a mixed bag of men, women and children, who lifted up their voices, and the roof, with a will. When the new organ was installed father had caused an inscription to be painted across it in Latin, to the effect that it is Love, not Noise, which reaches the heart of God. He should have appended a translation!

In the old days, long before our time, there was a minstrel's gallery, and a clerk who gave out the hymns and notices. One day, so it is said, he announced that the choir would now sing, 'Who is the King of Glory?' and a voice from the gallery was heard to say 'Pass up the rosin Joe, and us'll show'em who be the King of Glory.'

The cottage question was always a burning one, and a great many of those in existence were quite unfit for human, or even animal habitation. Father minced no words about them with the landlords, threatenig them with the alternative of the Sanitary Inspector or an epidemic of typhoid.
The Sanitary Inspector could do no more than condemn here and condemn there, but little or nothing was accomplished, and happily a typhoid epidemic did not materialise either. All that happened in fact was that the Coope's, grown-ups and children were not bidden to the two great houses where father had spoken his mind, but the ladies did bow to mother from their carriages, considering I suppose that she was more sinned against than sinning.

All the water in Thurlestone had to be drawn from a covered well in the village, and carried home in two pails on a wooden yoke. We had our own well at the Rectory, but it took an hour to pump the tank full up in the attics so we had to be very careful of water, especially in summer when the rain water tank was running low. Our nightly bath in front of the nursery fire was on the instalment plan, youngest first, and so on until the eldest lowered herself into a veritable pea soup of sandy, soapy water, hotted up for her by an addition from the brown enamel can standing near.

At the top of the village a tap ran off the same spring that fed the well, and sitting on it on fine days on his little camp chair, was old Pound, smoking a clay pipe and exchanging yarns with whoever stopped to speak to him. Mrs.Pound kept the sweet shop and supported herself and her husband who was so crippled with rheumatics that he could only just crawl down to the tap with the help of a couple of walking sticks, and there he stayed, hour in, hour out.

It was reputed to be old Pound who, when another stranger shouted out'You old Johnny there, where can I get a decent night's lodging?' replied quietly, 'Well, there be Kingsbridge Workhouse, Sparkhall Lynatic Asylum, and Exeter Gaol, all suitable I reckon.'

Good manners in Devon are natural, and courtesy is given and expected. It never struck us as odd that father should never fail to sweep off his hat when he met his own little daughters in the lanes, any more than that he should do so to the old goodies pattering along in their clogs on their way to the well with the yoke and pails. Nor were we ever allowed to go into the cottages without knocking and being invited in, and of course (although some people cannot see the point of this) we were never permitted to speak dialect to the cottagers. We spoke it among ourselves when we felt inclined, but not as a rule, and I was surprised and puzzled when I got to boarding school in Berkshire and the other girls asked how it was that I spoke ordinary English so well.

John got into terrible disgrace once when he was about five, for he sat on the low wall outside the hotel and abused the visitors' children in broad Devon, so that they were too frightened to go past him. I don't expect he said anything more than 'Yu gurt toads' or something of that sort, but he alarmed them by his menancing air, and the hotel wall was put out of bounds, and John got beaten. Dad with a slipper was no joke!

Father used to say that Donald Ilbert would fill a book, and he certainly had a volume of memories about Donald, who was his church warden, and also the son of the Rev. Courtenay Peregrine Ilbert who had built our Rectory and bought up his own children there.

Donald was a 'simple' soul, and Thurlestone his only possible environment, where everyone knew and loved him and to whom he was still Master Donald when well up in the eighties.

He was proud of being born the same day as the Duke of Connaught, and liked you to know it. When he was pleased he would rub his hands together with a noise like sandpaper, and chuckle, and we children used to like him to win at cards or quoits or croquet because it meant much more to him than it did to us, and he would nearly rub his hands off.

He was an upright and good gentleman and if he was not blessed with the sharpest of wits, he played his part in our village with loyalty and distinction, and father never repented having asked him to be Rector's Churchwarden, wanting as he did to pay respect to the Ilbert family through Donald. So certain lapses from the narrow path during church services would not invite criticism or censure, but amused tolerance, and father would chuckle over 'dear old Donald' and his little ways. He had his own seat at the top of the church with the warden's rod at his elbow and the collection bag ready to hand. This handing round of the bag would sometimes surprise visitors, because he set himself a time limit, and if you fumbled or hesitated he would shake it right in your face, hissing 'hurry up, hurry up, can't you?', while to his own sister Mrs. Robert Campbell, he was not even so polite, turning in despair to the congregation and exclaiming 'Bless the woman, I can't wait here all day'.

When father mounted the pulpit Donald would carefully take out his hunter watch and lay it open before him, leaning forward slightly and gazing intently at it. Then when the twenty minutes were up which he regarded as the outside limit, he would pick up the watch, give an enormous groan, and snap it to with a loud click. Father would compress his lips, and say hastily, 'Lastly'... and Donald would relax, but not altogether.

It was a joy to us when Donald's sister Miss Helen Ilbert would join us for bathing at Yarmer sands, across the golf links and through the rushes. It was safe bathing here, and we knew that we must avoid Broadsands, the next cove, while Lea Foot was rather deep for the little ones. So we generally went to Yarmer and donned our queer blue cotton combinations, reaching well below the knees, and buttoning up under our chins. Miss Ilbert had a smart creation, not faded like ours, but a rich dark blue bunting very full in the legs, and ending in frills round her ankles ornamented with white braid. Thus clad she would cast herself into the ocean and swim strongly around to our great admiration. We had no tent and simply used the clefts in the rocks, and hung our clothes around on pieces that stuck out. Once when there was a high sea running and Miss Ilbert had taken me down alone, she decided to risk it and we went over by the Lion Rock where the water was quieter. Even so it was not quiet enough for me, and a wave caught me and flung me against her but she managed to grasp me safely and together we floundered ashore, deciding to call it a day. Miss Ilbert's day had not finished though, because in banging against her I had given her two black eyes, and my shame and sorrow were great.

There is a stream which runs out at Yarmer, over the side of the cliff, and when it is running low it simply disappears into the sands, and is no more seen. But on a winter's day or in spring, we used to spend hours there damming it with wet sand and stones, making lakes with rivers running from them to more lakes, and the more imaginative ones would bring flowers and foliage form the cliffs and fashion Japanese gardens, with tiny stone bridges crossing the rivers, and trees of sea thistle.

Whatever the weather there was always a good attendance at church, and when the summer visitors came, it was packed to capacity. Chairs were brought from here there and anywhere and filled up the aisles so that there was barely room to walk up them. The space under the tower, the chancel by the choir stalls, the steps of the font, all were filled up and still more room was wanted. Donald used to dash up and down with an angry face, beckoning here and pointing there, his face streamig with perspiration, and willing helpers would go out to scour around for yet more chairs. And as the church filled, so did the heat increase, in spite of open doors, and plenty of them there were,

the south door, the Lady Chapel, the north door, the belfry door, and the vestry, but the fresh air that came in was hot too, and we sweltered. At last Donald, having deposited the last contingent on hassocks by the lectern, threw in his hand, and standing on the chancel steps, addressed the multitude.
'Drat you people', he cried, 'Why will you come to church?'. Then father emerged in his cassock from the vestry and took matters in charge, filling up the choir stalls and the seats in the porch, while Miss Waddington, who had taken over the choir from mother, struck up the opening voluntary, and peace desended. A bumble bee droned, the minute bell was sounding, and the Cromwellian clock gave a wheezy click and proceeded to tell us that it was eleven o'clock. Enter father again, and a great uprising and downsitting heralded the opening of Mattins. Some fell by the wayside and tottered out sooner or later with green faces, but on the whole we stood it well, and what a collection!

Those years ago our village possessed that most golden of possessions - silence. It brooded over the cottage gardens and the village street, in the quiet coves, the lanes and the deep valleys, but there was music too in the sighing of the sea, rustle of the trees, the sudden singing of feathers as a gull swooped past your head. But this music came to you intermittently between the silence, so perhaps you noticed the music more keenly, and only when you went away to city life and to the noise that is not music to country ears, then only did you realise that the great and ancient quiet of an old village is the song in your heart,

The sounds of Thurlestone were lovely ones, and surely the only melody that can be exquisite even though it is out of tune is that of church bells. Our five bells were not in tune, yet father always said that the tenor bell had the sweetest tone of any in Devon, and when I hear a peal that is tone perfect I have a feeling that anything so right cannot be quite right, and that the mingled sob of the imprisoned peal in a belfry is the perfect discord.

The music of Thurlestone started for us with the first cawing of the rooks in the elms up the drive, and the squeaking bough of one tree that overlapped another. Neither of them would give way, so year after year they leant against each other and complained with a high, thin note every time the wind blew. Then a farm cart would go up the road with a creak, and the slow clip-clop of the old horse taking his time about it and not being persuaded otherwise. A scuttering of padded feet heralded the cows going to be milked, and we would hear Jim Bevell chanting in a sing-song voice 'here we come down; here we come down'. Later on we knew we should hear the same scuttering of feet, and Jim would be singing to his herd 'here we come up; here we come up'.

Our stable yard was cobbled, and the sound of the pony being led out to be harnessed, with her iron shoes ringing on the rounded stones, was the moment to hurry if you were going out in the trap. Father spoilt his ponies more than he did his children and we were never allowed to keep the pony waiting. Dora was patient and did not punish us, but Belle was always in a hustle to be off, and if she had to stand by the front door longer than she liked, she would pay you out when she felt your weight on the step at the back. Before there was time for you to yank yourself into the seat and seize the reins, Belle would back quickly and obliquely into the wall of the house, and then if she did not suceed in crushing you to death, she took a leap forward and galloped up the drive, turning at right angles out of the gate as if the devil were on her tail.

None of us were ever hurt, but we were often badly scared, and so must have been those in the roadway as Jehu flashed by. We did not flash for long though, for the hill started to rise steeply about fifty yards off, and Belle would suddenly drop to a wearisome, dawdling walk, as if absolutely exhausted by the long wait in the drive and the inconsiderate behaviour of the young person at the reins.

In those days the women wore pattens over their shoes to go to and from the pump with their pails, and they made a peculiar sound which is best described by the word itself. How nice such words are, and how ugly the word which describes them. I love shiver, and clink, and boom and hiss. Splutter is a good one; so is tantrum, and lazy, and cavern. Especially cavern, for you can hear the echo of your voice dying away in a hollow undertone just as it would in a cavern.

Crash - that word itself transports me to Lea Foot on a stormy day when the Atlantic rollers have become enraged, and great breakers are rearing up with white horses frilling their edges, as they gather speed and come towards, uplifted in menace. But they miss you again and again, and crash with their power expended on the stony shingle just below where you stand, only to rush back with a deadly under suction to gather momentum for the next spring, leaping and tearing through the rocks, foaming with anger ..... Crash!

In such weather seaweed piles up in stacks, and if it is the variety known to us as horses' tails, there will soon be a cart lumbering down to the tide mark to garner the precious stuff and haul it away to manure the fields. Father used to have a load every year for his asparagus beds, and the stench of it when it matured in the hot sun was the only thing that would keep us out of the kitchen when father and the gardener were safely elsewhere. A high wall of cob surrounded this garden, and the door into it by the stables was kept locked, for eleven very good reasons, for although we got plenty of fruit to eat, we were never satisfied. My own method was simple, as the light six-foot ladder was within my strength to carry, and once up on the top of the wall I could pull it up and let it down the other side with ease. Taking a basket never entered my head, because for one thing if I were caught, the basket would be evidence enough to hang me. But I felt honour bound (since honour had to come into it somewhere) to take back enough for those outside, so the obvious place was the legs of my blue cotton bloomers, conventiently held at the knees with elastic. Stuffed with ripe peaches, greengages and golden plums, I had to walk carefully to avoid crushing, and the anxious ascent of the wall and safe arrival down the other side was full of suspense for me and mine.

Father must have guessed that someone was stealing the fruit, because I never stinted and only the best was good enough, but he never asked me, or anyone else, about it, and continued to padlock the walled garden as soon as the gardener went home. Mother never asked questions either when I approached her with a blushing peach, warm in its prime, and put into her hand.

An extra trace horse would come down to the shore while the seaweed cart was being loaded, and even then it was all the two of them could do to drag the heavy weight up the shelving shore to the road by the golf house. The wheels were deeply sunk into the shingle, and the horses would strain and tug and strain again before they could get going, with the carter putting his shoulder to the wheel and shouting encouragement to Boxer and Daisy, while we threw our puny weights in at the back and imagined we were helping. At last they struggled on the mettalled road and made their steady way home, with a merciful rest on the steep corner of the hill by Drury Lane. (Miss Drury lived down it!) Then with a heave they're off again, harness creaking and the chain trace going rattle-tattle against the shafts, and so on and up until they reach their destination where with a tip and a heave backwards their shining slippery load of brown seaweed, rich in iodine, is tipped and stacked. Boxer blows contentedly through his nostrils and stands quietly in the shafts as Daisy is led out of the traces and re-harnessed to her own waiting cart. Daisy has been a friend in deed and in need.

When the nights were breathless with heat, and sleep seemed far away, Hilda, Wins and I would lie on our little iron bedsteads, blankets flung off, looking for pictures in the branches of the elm trees in the drive, and when darkness fell and a kindly breeze fluttered the curtains and stroked our hot foreheads with cool fingers, then we would hear a sound of Thurlestone that we listened and waited for night after night - the young men of the village coming home from their cider and ale, singing as they came, with accordions and mouth organs setting the tune. It was harmonious singing, not raucous or drunken, and the songs they sang were the old ones, songs we knew too, and our small voices would chime in very softly with "Oh dear, what can the matter be", as they passed by our garden wall into the village, and so to their own homes, and quiet fell upon us and them. But the melody that rings louder and truer in my memory than any other is on the dark winter nights, with the oil lamps burning in a gentle glow, and a wood fire of apple sending blue and purple flames licking up the chimney. Then mother is sitting relaxed at her piano, and her small white hands, with a stretch I could never attain, are weaving magic for her entranced little girls upstairs. Wealth we had not, nor position, nor prospects, but we went to sleep enriched by the strains of Liszt's Consolations, and were lapped in the beauty of those sweet sounds.

Storms there were, and terror by night when the sou'wester roared and shouted, and the sea became a demented cruel monster, thirsting for the souls of men and ships. Then it was that we knelt and prayed for all those at sea tonight, and prayed with all our hearts, for those who live their lives by the sea fear it as well as love it, when it goes mad on a winter's night we know that brave men are in danger.

Brave men not only on the sea but also on the shore; the coastguards at watch on the cliffs, ready to summon help and to give it, together with the lifeboat men who, in our day, manned their boat at Hope Cove, and had not then the protection and the benefit of the breakwater. They had to launch her right into the waves, generally in a high gale and often with the tide running strongly against them. But the rocket signal of distress in Bigbury Bay was enough for them, and somehow or another - most of the able-bodied villagers lending a hand - the lifeboat would take the water and the crew bend to their oars with strength and determination.

The explosion of a rocket at sea would get us all out of bed, peering through the windows for the sight of another, which would give us some idea where the wreck was. Generally it would be on the reef of rocks running across the bay well inside the tip of Bolt Tail, and known and avoided by mariners, but sometimes in those days of sail the running sea andthe lashing gale took command,and then it was that the rockets flared and shot skywards, and the good men of Hope answered the cry for help.

Which brings me to another sound, the first motor-car to come down the village. Afar off we heard this chuff-chuff-rattle-rattle, and as it was coming nearer all the time we hung out over the gate bars to see what the noise meant. The chariot hove in view, leaving swirls and clouds of dust in its wake, and came charging down the village hell for leather, at about fifteen miles an hour. If this was not enough, another thrill was sitting in the back, someone we had never expected to see in Thurlestone.

There he was, neat in his Dartmouth uniform, his golden head shining, his white teeth gleaming as he laughed with his friends, and all too soon it was over and he had gone. But we had seen him, our own Edward, Prince of Wales, come to

Thurlestone for a game of golf and tea at the hotel. He often came again, and sometimes brought 'young Bertie' with him, and we always festooned the garden gate as the dust cloud approached and he with it. It became a solemn point of honour that whoever heard the car first should rush around the garden shouting 'Motor Car', and not go up the drive until everyone had been summoned, but there was usually plenty of time to do this because the car made such a devil of a row that we heard it at least a mile off.

In the twenty-five years we lived at Thurlestone we had four different gardeners, and the first comes first with me and always will, Roger Jackman, the dearest friend a child could have, so patient with our rampaging around and so tender and understanding when we were in disgrace elsewhere. A fall and a cut knee would take you to 'Jackun' for comfort, and he was always ready with a bruised dock leaf to rub over limbs stinging and smarting from nettles. Jackun had his own ideas about conduct, and a reproof from him 'Now then, none of that there. You behave vitty (proper) or else I'll send you indoors, so I will', would always have the desired effect. Jackun was an old fashioned gardener and did not by any means approve of any innovation father migh be minded upon, such as sowing in trenches to avoid having to water over-much, and once he was moved to address father, so great was his opposition to an order given, 'Coming along and interfering in my garden' was how he put it, and father's laughter was not understood or appreciated. He thought a lot of us, 'my children to Rectory' and his bon mot, often repeated down the years, was'when you've seen one, you've seen the lot'. He worked hard for us, too hard in fact, and the time came when his heart became affected due, father regretfully believed, to the effort of pumping the water from the well to the house. He had to leave us and take life easy at his home in West Buckland, but as we went down to school there every day we used to gallop along to the cottage and call out 'Is Jackun there?' many days of the week. He had such nice blue eyes and really fine features, and when one day we were sent to the cottage during break to see Jackun, we knew it was to say goodbye to him as he lay in his great bed in the whitewashed room, with Dorothy his daughter fanning him as he struggled for breath that was failing. We were not frightened or even over-awed, but kissed him with the love that his love had engendered in us, and tip-toed away.

One of the nicest gravestones in Thurlestone churchyard is that of Roger Jackman's, in stone with a pattern of fruit and flowers carved around it, and the words 'well done thou good and faithful servant'. Father designed it and had it specially made, and on the grave was our own cross which we children filled with flowers every week until we went away from Thurlestone.

Our next gardener was so good looking that he set the heart of our nurse a-fluttering, and we were greatly impressed when we were on holiday at Yealmpton one summer, and Frank arrived on his bicycle all the way from Thurlestone to see our pretty Lillian. It cannot be more than twenty-five miles, but hard going in Devon, and it was our first glimpse of true love in blossom, we did not allow them one moment alone together but hung around with popping eyes to see what next. However, courting in those days was a very respectable affair and started with yarding, which simply meant that you either walked or sat, three feet apart. Arming came next, and that meant business, because you armed in public and everyone could believe the evidence of their eyes. What followed was not always in the book of rules, and then it was that the bride wore blue, (and the church bells were silent!) but Frank and Lillian did not make that mistake, and the bride wore white.

Our conduct up and down the village was of course a source of comment, and we were pretty careful not to offend, for if we did we would have to run the gauntlet of Mrs. Pound at the top, then Mrs. Toms, then Sarah Masters, followed by Mrs Rose Bevell and finally Miss Ellus. At some time or another we had come under their special wing, and that constituted in their sight, and in ours, the right to scold, correct and criticise our goings out and our comings in.

When Thurlestone was 'discovered', and we had to share our small heaven with beastly visitors, father found a new source of income, and he reckoned that by letting the Rectory for six weeks or so in the summer, he could pay the boarding school fees of one child. It meant leaving the peaches behind for our tenants, but we soon forgot that in the new joys of Dartmoor, or the village life of Yealmpton and Brixton, near Plymouth.

The Glebe Cottage, set in the Rectory wall, was in a sad state of disrepair, so father had it pulled down and built a new one, a pretty gabled dwelling with a good living room and airy bedrooms. Here came the Hills to live and work for us, with their children, Albert, Harold and Rosalind. Harold was a young tearaway then, and we used to follow his devilries with bated and admiring breath. He grew up into a fine young fellow, and lost his life in World War One. Albert survived, and became a signalman on the then Great Western Railway, but he too was fated to a sudden death, being killed by an express train on the main line at Cornwood, just as he was handing over the Right of Way Key to an engine driver in the up Line. Rosalind in due time became our maid at the Rectory, and has remained one of our dearest friends through all the years that have past.

Laughter - oh what a release from tension and worry, and this singled out my father from among his fellows. He had such an appreciation for the ridiculous; such a savour for an amusing anecdote, and *joie de vivre* at all times. Mother only had to say 'One of you children run up to the village and tell father dinner is ready', so up you went to the village pump and stood and listened. Where you heard laughter, there would be father; so right to the hilarious cottage you sped, to find dad comfortably settled in the kitchen, chortling and chuckling as the quick Devonian repartee kept everyone in fits.

Father had a fund of 'Clergy Stories' which he would recount to visiting 'Guinea Pigs' - (so called becaue a locum tenens would get a guinea a service). One we loved and knew by heart was about the Bishop staying in the Rectory after taking a Confirmation Service. We then had a boot-boy . . . (first thing before school), and he was chosen to take up the Bishop's hot water can and shaving mug to the spare room. He was told to knock on the door, and when the Bishop called 'come in', to go in quietly, say 'Good-Mornin' My Lord'; then put the can in the basin and cover it with the felt muff, and retire. BUT, when he knocked and waited outside, the Bishop called out 'Who is it?' Alfie lost his head entirely, and replied in clarion tones, 'IT'S THE LORD, MY BOY'. Of course this went the whole round of the Diocese of Exeter, and many upright parish priests have since claimed it as their own.

Winter at Thurlestone had for us one compensation; it was

all ours, as there were no visitors. The links and the cliffs, the beaches and coves, they were ours again, our very own. Apart from an occasional nasty east wind it was never really cold, and until I went away to school I had never seen snow falling. Snowdrops were out by the second or third week in January, and we never failed to pick a bunch surrounded by small ivy leaves, and take them up to old Mrs. Ilbert for her birthday on January 16th. Once Mr. Frank Hewitt, our local artist, did skate gingerly up and down the Lea Pond but that was an event not repeated in our time.

Thurlestone Church was falling down, or at least it would have already fallen down were it not for mighty baulks of timber holding up the crumbling walls. The tower itself inclined inland, but had long since adapted itself to the souwesterly gales, and was probably safer at the present angle than before. Father, eager for fresh fields to conquer, would not rest until the church had been restored, and continued to collect for a Church Restoration Fund in his tiny parish of four hundred souls, forming a committee with Mr. Chandos-Pole as Treasurer, and confidently expecting the hundreds and thousands to roll in. Roll in they did, in trickles, over a number of years, and people would say laughingly, Rector can get money out of stones. We had bazaars, concerts, plays, all of which we got up ourselves.

A Church Bazaar in our garden, given on a fine day, attracted plenty of people from outside the parish; for one reason, there was little enough of organised entertainment in those days, and one met old friends and acquaintances, and had a magnificent tea for sixpence. Cleaning up for the "Feet" was Jackman's main concern for weeks beforehand in the garden, and paths would be weeded, beds dug, lawns mown and swept, until our tangled acres looked like the grounds of a prosperous mansion. We always had a lovely show of flowers in the Ash walk, below the terrace, where sub-tropical plants grew and flourished, figs ripened in the sunshine, and honeysuckle blossomed early in Spring. Mr. Hill, once a London policeman, was installed at the front gates to take the admission money, and the stalls were set out on the big lawn, fancy, china and glass, sweets, toys, bran pie, and what you will. Mrs. Chandos-Pole always had the sweet stall, beautiflly decorated with bright strips of crepe paper, and she would dress in gay clothing and a marvellous hat from Woolands, all to match. Round on the little lawn would be a putting green, and here too would be produced the piece de resistance, a play. Generally it was the Mad Hatter's Tea Party which never seemed to pall; we did it year after year, and still they paid to see it.

Of course the time came when other houses were built in the parish and other friends came to share its life with us. We viewed them with grave suspicion at first, but wise parents soon brought us together at picnics and tea-parties, and they ceased to be 'foreigners', sharing our haunts and hobbies.

I suppose the first were the Harcourts who built Aune Cross at Aunemouth, right the other end of the parish, and about a mile up river; Dadie Harcourt was much the same age as Wins, who spent a lot of time there, sometimes sharing her lessons, and at all times her special friend; Cecil Harcourt, who we called Jock, was our hero, then a Dartmouth cadet, and we eyed him with respect and some quickened heartbeats. He tolerated us very kindly, but was beyond our silly games.

When the Clarks came from Canada to the Whiddons at Bantham we were sent down to Bantham sands with our tea to meet them for the first time, and hadn't the faintest idea what they would look like, but we knew that they were called Hilda and Frances. At last we spied two little girls, but one of them had a black face, and we had a moment of horror. We had to brave it out, and Wins and I approached nearer, only to find that the younger girl had a big black veil over her face. It was Frances, always delicate, and I suppose her mother wanted to keep the sand out of her lungs, but it was a shock to us at first sight. Frances was great fun, and she and I became tremendous friends, having the same naughty idea of humour, spending hours 'fishing' for old boots and tin cans over the side of the disused lime-kiln in their garden. She did not survive her adolesence, and it was my first real sadness.

Then there were the Ritchies, mother and son, who built Kennedy opposite the church; Arthur was about fourteen when they first came to Thurlestone, with lustrous dark hair, and lustrous dark eyes. He was a serious-minded studious lad, but he used to join our cricket matches and one day we cut his eye open with a fast ball. This was very bad, because he was the only son of his mother, and she was a widow, so it would have been far better if the ball had hit one of us, who had so many eyes between us. However, Mrs. Ritchie took it very well and Arthur's lustrous eye was none the worse.

When Kennedy was finished and they moved in Arthur started an aquarium up in the attic and became a naturalist. Once I was invited up to witness the birth of some sea slugs, which emerged from their mother's body one after the other, but we were supremely unselfconscious about such matters and I followed the progress of the little family with much interest. He kept his sea creatures in beautiful condition and was to us a familiar figure on the sea shore with his nets and pots searching for more.

When he grew up and went away and Kennedy was his no longer, he used to come back sometimes and see us, and then it was that Joan and Gwen felt for him the same fascination that we had and would festoon themselves around him, clinging to his neck and arms, and making a perfect nuisance of themselves. Arthur stood it like a man and would stagger round the garden with those two small dumplings hanging on to him like his own limpets of the olden days. (Now Professor Ritchie, Dundee University).

Ball Park on the Buckland Road was a wild field with bracken, bluebells, a quarry and masses of blackberries. Being on our way home from school, it was a natural playground for us and we heard with horror one day that it was sold and we must not go there any more. Hm, we thought, and continued to go there until at long last a building began to rise on the crest of the field and we knew that paradise was lost. So the Grey House was built, and three gorgeous boys came to live there, Peter, Jack and Geoff Inchbald. Gosh, they were rich - at least to our standards. Their mother wore soft silk dresses with high lace necks and carried a parasol to church, and Auntie Tom who lived with them then wore lovely suits which seemed to have grown on her.

Naturally enough we gradually got to know these superb boys, who were really human beings after all and asked us to meet them at their boathouse at Bantham and fish for crabs with pieces of tough cake tied on to string. We soon got over any idea that they were too grand for us, and had some fine fishing expeditions and parties with progressive games in the winter, book teas, and once hide and seek in the moonlight in our garden. I think it was that which finished it, for their mother was in the drawing room with our mother, and we were evidently having a high old time in the garden, although believe it or not, not the high old time she seemed to suspect. Anyway after that the spell was broken and our innocent friendships with it, for the next holidays we were rather obviously not so welcome as we had been and became self-conscious when we met.

Down a steep hill and up the other side is West Buckland, and there in a fair sized cottage with a big garden lived our Aunt Amy, father's only sister. We walked there every day, wet or fine, to do our lessons with her, for our so-called governesses were not engaged to teach us, but to act as our keepers when we were to old for a nurse.

We loved our lessons with Aunt Amy, who gave us a half-holiday every Wednesday, which we sent entirely with her. In the winter we played games in her tiny parlour, where she kept a wonderful games cupboard to which she added whenever anything new or exciting came on the market. In the summer we picked her up at Buckland, and laden with a gorgeous tea, set forth to Bantham sands. Generally we had our tea in the Roman Camp on the sand dunes, and although grown-ups often found real Roman pottery and precious relics there, yet I, for all my digging with my little wooden spade, never found a thing.

Our education was father's great concern; the elder ones were at boarding schools, but we younger ones had to be provided for, so he engaged two sisters, the Misses Phillips who came to live in T'Amy's cottage, and set up a private school to which we went, together with Hilda and Frances Clark from Bantham, and Una and Margie Stidston from Thurlestone. Other children came and went, but our little lot was the backbone of the school, and we were certainly well grounded in essentials. The Phillips were followed by Mrs. and Miss Webb, and Miss Webb was distinguished by having a jaw which would suddenly give a loud crack, and stay in a queer position. Miss Webb would hurry out of class and come back later looking rather pained, but with her jaw in the right line once more.

It was a point of honour that we ran all the way home from

school, but if you know Buckland Hill you might not believe me. We never drove the pony down or up it, and a farm cart could only get down with drags on the wheels, and the carter holding back the straining horse by sheer force of his own body. We even went as far to tie treacle tins on our feet with string through holes made with nails, and clip clop down the hill that way. With treacle tins you could walk right through the stream in the valley instead of going over the stone bridge like a little lady.

Turn to Bantham, past Rockhill, then through the field gate to the footpath that crosses the crest of the hill and falls steeply to Bantham Lea. Here you have a superb view of the western side of Bigbury Bay, with Burgh island at the mouth of the river Avon, and on a fine day the long and the short of Eddystone Lighthouse, the short being of course the stump of the old lighthouse. The upper part stands on Plymouth Hoe now, but don't ask me how it got there.

We cross the lea and climb again up a narrow path that can be the hottest spot in the wide world on a windless day, and so we come to the Sloop Inn, and Bantham hamlet. Thatched whitewashed cottages run in an unbroken line from the Sloop to the last cottage at the gate to the Ham, which is a ham-shaped grassy headland ending in a knuckle at Jenkins' boathouse where the river runs into the sea under the opposite high cliffs of Bigbury. The little river is wide and tidal here, with a narrow strong current which will get you into difficulties if you try to scull across it without knowing that you must go hard upstream if you want to land opposite where you started.

Bantham sands, way across the Ham, are a paradise for anyone, with rocks and pools, shells, and sheltered nooks, and a protecting power which jealously guards its amenities and limits the numbers of campers. Beware of leaving litter about, or broken bottles, someone will be after you, and next time you won't find it so easy to get through the gate for your day's pleasure. Up the river about a mile is Stiddicombe Creek, nice for picnics, and the copse has the biggest outsize in primroses ever picked.

Sometimes in the old days you saw a small procession of boats proceeding up river to the strawberry gardens, and in those boats were the Ilberts, the Ritchies, the Harcourts, the Coopes, all with large baskets and large appetites. We picked our strawberries ourselves and had them weighed when we had got enough, having also been wisely allowed to eat as many as we could cram in while we picked. The fall of the tide determined our time to turn for home, and having disembarked again at Bantham we would start the climb to Thurlestone, taking it in turn to carry the baskets, but not eating so many now.

But while we are still down at Bantham father will say, 'Look, he's a Bantham man alright', and those in the know realise that he has spied a large patch on the Bantham man's trousers. The explanation is simple, the Sloop Inn boasts wooden benches for its customers, and the Thurlestone inn none at all, so a Bantham man wears his trousers out in a good cause.

And from the Sloop Inn we naturally come to Harry, who has a story all of his own.

Come back fifty years or so, and find him comfortably leaning against the bank overlooking the sea and sands. Harry smokes his shag and thinks of nothing in particular. It is a hot, sleepy afternoon, and he lazily watches the holidaymakers below paddling and bathing, shrimping in the rocky pools, or just like him, doing naught. It suits Harry, so long as his brother Fred will let him earn a bit when he feels inclined by driving the bakery van and delivering the fresh loaves, the Devon tough-cakes, and the halfpenny buns rich in currants and smelling of good yeast.

Red-haired Harry is tall, big-boned, ruddy-skinned and with something of grace about him that one must recognise as breeding. Two of Harry's interests are cider and love-making, the Sloop bar and a pretty maid making up his heaven on earth. Indeed, the very moment we happen upon him behind the bank on the Ham he is waiting for Gertie, whose afternoon off it is. Gertie is very willing for a bit of sweethearting while she is down here for the summer holidays, dull enough otherwise for a nursemaid in a furnished house. Harry is never true in love - here today and gone tomorrow, but while it lasts it is the real thing, and he is a persuasive lover.

So he waits patiently for Gertie and puffs at his pipe while the gulls scream and swirl overhead, and the happy cries of the children on the sands below are wafted up the cliffs to the bank where the green hummocks of sea thrift diffuse a delicious scent from their pink tufts of flowers.

A murmur of approaching voices reaches him and he peeps cautiously over the bank. Two young girls are coming down Ham path, strangers to Harry, but he eyes them appreciatively as they pause and look up at the notice above the lifebelt and rope which have been there as long as he can remember. They read the notice and one of them laughs, although what there is to laugh about Harry cannot understand.

'If you bathe to the left of this notice, you will probably be drowned.'

Nothing funny there surely, but maids be silly toads, and where is that Gertie all this while? Harry shifts to a more comfortable position, and allows the torpor invading his sun-soaked limbs to engulf him completely. Harry sleeps. He wakes again to the cries of the children on the sands, but to something more than that. There is terror, horror, anguish in those cries, and mingled with them are the shouts of the men, and desperate screams of women. Harry somehow becomes transformed as he leaps to his feet and jumps the bank in almost a single movement, to see below him a sight which momentarily freezes him with shock. There are five -six -seven - no, eight people struggling against the deadly current to the left of the notice board, and they are being swept around the rocks towards the point and the open sea. On the fringe of the water stand the agonised on-lookers, the demented children shrieking, and some of the women covering their faces with their hands, but Harry waits for no more as he seizes the coil of rope and sets off down the sand dunes faster than he has ever run before.

'Follow me, sir ... Follow me, sir', he shouts as he races to the far corner of the sands, and the men folk follow his lead as he climbs over rocks, across gullies, running, leaping, scrambling, to get to the point before it is too late. Harry becomes a God, inspired, uplifted. He gives orders, throws out the rope as he girds one end round his waist, and then he leaps into the sea.

The human chain he has formed behind him play out the rope as he swims strongly and steadily towards the death trap, his eyes ever intent on that group of struggling, sinking, exhausted human souls.

So, at last, he reaches the first, and hauls up the half-drowned girl whom one of them is supporting (where has he seen her before?) and then, in firm, ringing, confident tones, he cries out

'You'm all right, don't worry, no one; hold on to the rope, and hold on tight. Us'll pull ye in, all the lot of ye'.

One by one he hauls them to the firm tautness of the guiding rope, diving for one, clipping another on the chin, as he avoids the clutch of despair that means death for both of them; one by one he shepherds them on to that rope, and all the time, over there on the rocks, the human chain pulls steadily, surely, and all the children cease to scream and stand mutely watching, while the women begin to thank God with fearful hope. Now they are safely brought in, half- drowned, choked and spent, but alive, everyone of them. Harry can no longer see or stand or even breathe; he is the last to be pulled in and collapses there on the rocks, retching, gasping and sobbing, his saturated clothing clinging to his great frame, with garlands of seaweed streaming from the wet disorder of his tangled hair. Harry cuts an unheroic figure, but a hero lies there.

Later on the father of the girl who has laughed at the notice board, and to save whom seven gallant men and women, and Harry, had nearly gone to their death, later on the father thanks them very nicely and presents Harry with a cigar and a golden ten-shilling piece, but Harry is not all that grateful because it transpires that Gertie was fair put out to find him gone, and will have none of him when he tries to explain.

Other heads were put together, and one fine day a fine watch and chain, with inscription, are handed to Harry, together with a goodly sum of money invested under the care of a local worthy who, while sharing the general view that Harry is a grand chap, none better, also agrees that it would be a pity for that tidy bit of cash to dissapate down Harry's throat in the form of fermented apple juice. So the money is to be held in trust, but everyone knows that Harry will treasure the watch and chain even above the love of women.

When I was fourteen a serious financial misfortune befell us; the firm which leased father's London property going bankrupt and depriving him for some years of his private income. By this time the elder members were in training, and the youngest being taught at home, while we middle ones were all away at boarding school. Father lost the power to sleep and mother became a worried wraith, but somehow we muddled through. Thanks to Miss Helen Ilbert, Arthur was able to stay up at

Oxford and take his degree and John was kept on at Radley. I was working for matriculation, and as soon as I had that behind me was to be sent to the Leipzig Conservatoire for a musical career. Everyone in a position to do so came to the rescue, and though I had to say goodbye forever to Leipzig, I stayed on at school and earned my own way by teaching the junior school music. I had not the faintest idea how to teach, and having been obliged to give up my own lessons, and no time alloted for practice, I took every opportunity of sitting at the piano myself and showing my willing pupils how it should be done! Having got through my exam I left school at sixteen and spent the next year at home and taught the three youngest their lessons in the old night nursery, now their school room. I must say they were very good and I tried to follow in Miss Ilbert's footsteps and make the lessons into adventurous experiences, but I doubt if they learned very much. In the holidays I did the cooking to help mother who never liked it, but it was only too easy, for we were cut down to meat once a week, no fish from Grimsby, and bread and cheese and cocoa ad nauseam. It was a grim time for all of us, for we realised that we were down to the knuckle. John took it very hard and went to father and asked if he could leave school and go to work as a jobbing gardener, but it did not come to that, although the offer was appreciated.

Our first big separation came soon, when Arthur passed into the Malayan Civil Service and sailed away. We did not see him again for five years. Katherine was at the Morland Institute, and Mary training as a games mistress. Hilda was at a children's hospital, and Wins was undetermined and doing odd jobs. Just as well she did, because Owen Webb came back from India and married her. 'There's one jam pot fallen off the shelf' said the village, who by this time were watching our little affairs with keen attention. Not that they were many or in the least spectacular - there were very few young men around, and I don't blame them if they fought shy of the nine girls who went around in droves and always seemed happy enough in each other's company. We must have been formidable, and mother, overworked and preoccupied, was not in a position to entertain, and anyway husband hunting for her daughters never entered her head. By the time we left Thurlestone Wins was still the only married one, and the jam pots fell off the shelf very slowly indeed.

The decision to leave our old home was a hard one for father to make. He would have liked to have laid his bones at Thurlestone, but the hard fact remained that here they were, still in low water, with the big house and enormous garden, and all their children had left home to earn their livings. Mother was like a distracted hen with no chicks, and was frankly miserable, knowing full well that they could not even afford to send us our fares to come home for our holidays. Also the fabric of the Rectory was badly in need of substantial repair, and the roof was in a bad way, which was all father's responsibility. He made up his mind that this was the end. He and mother had come there solely for the sake of their children, and now they must leave for the sake of their children, and move nearer to London. I don't think we realised at first what a wrench it was going to be, for we missed our mother and father so much in our exile, that to have them within reach was easily the first consideration. The living of Thurlestone was accepted by a well-to-do bachelor, and the old house and garden knew us no more.

Father had done wonders, there can be no doubt about it. Besides restoring the church, he had built a new church school at the top of the village. He had rebuilt Glebe Cottage, and raised money for a Chapel of Ease at Bantham. He had seen the parish develop from a secluded outpost into a fashionable resort, and he had adapted himself to its growing needs. He and mother had brought up their children as they intended, content with simple pleasures that money cannot buy, and they left Thurlestone with the loving regret of everybody there. We were the Rectory children, but they were all that stands for kindness, sympathy, tolerance and good humour. No wonder that mother and father still stand for what Thurlestone was then, and still the heart of the Village beats strong and true and faithful to the days gone by.

Appendix
Thurlestone Families
by Dr NEVILLE C. OSWALD, F.R.C.P.

The Protestation Returns of 1641 for Thurlestone and the neighbouring parishes of Bigbury, Churchstow, South Milton and South Huish reveal many similar surnames, those most frequently mentioned being Hingston, Shepherd, Wakeham, Lidstone and Jarvis. These names figure prominently in the Thurlestone registers after 1650 and must have derived in part from marriages across parochial boundaries. The table shows the most prominent Thurlestone families during the 300 years, each having at least 150 entries in the baptism register. At the outset, a distinction must be made between surnames recorded as such and descendants through married daughters and hence having other surnames. This variable and often considerable difference may be seen by comparing, for example, Lidstone, Moore and Hardy where the original surname accounted for about two-thirds of the baptisms with the others where it represented far less. Account must also be taken of families new to the register whose relationship to those of the same name already there was sometimes uncertain. The simplest way to overcome this difficulty would seem to be to include all of a given surname, their descendants through male and female lines and new entries with the same original name.

Total baptisms, marriages and burials by name give the surest indications of the families already well established in 1650-99. Outstanding among them were Lidstone and Phillips, followed by Shepherd, Pilditch, Randall and Tabb.

Their descendants and others with the same surnames can be traced to 1850-99, during which the Lidstones and Phillips disappeared. The remainder continued into the twentieth century through married daughters at some stage, but all had lost their original names by then, their descendants being called Jackman (eight), Edgcombe (three), and Moore (two). Rather less well established in the early years were Worden (or Whiddon), Clark, Polybank, Crispin and Hingston. Many new families entered the parish over the years, but they rarely remained for more than two or three generations. Exceptions were the Moores and Hardys. Thename Moore first appeared in any of the registers in 1691 when John married Abigail Randall, a native of the parish. Theyhad 171 baptised descendants through nine generations, the last recorded being in 1939. Similarly, Hugh and Prothesa Hardy, whose marriage is not recorded, had their first child baptised in 1671 and then 150 descendants, the last in 1868. Indeed, these two marriages generated respectively no less than 71 and 84% of their total baptisms through their multiparous offspring. The Hannafords had an impact later, following the arrival of John and Honour in 1775.

The table does no more than set out the data in the baptism register. It cannot give the full story of intermarriage, for several reasons.

In the early years, especially before 1700, brides were occasionally entered by their Christian names only, sometimes followed by 'girl wife'. Although native born bridegrooms marrying elsewhere and returning to raise their families could usually be found in the baptism register, brides could not because their maiden names were not recorded. Some relationships were untraceable through the coincidence of similar names. These losses, although numerically small, may have had a considerable effect on family trees at times. For example, the marriage of John Moore to Abigail Randall credited each surname with 171 descendants, whereas Hugh Hardy had 150 descendants but the surname of his Prothesa is not known. Their marriage was not registered in Thurlestone, but there were Prothesas in the parish at the time, one of whom could have married Hugh. Variations such as these account for the big differences between total baptisms and baptisms by original surname in the table. The Randalls, Tabbs, and Wordens were all united at some stage with the rapidly proliferating Moores and Hardys.

The year 1777 was one of mixed fortunes for Thurlestone. Some of the rural industries of previous generations were in decline. The spinners and weavers, working in their cottages all over Devon, were becoming an increasing burden on parochial charities as a result of incessant wars, the loss of overseas markets for their wool and the beginnings of steam power from cheap coal in the woollen mills of Yorkshire and the Midlands. The cider trade, for which the South Hams was famous, was crippled when a tax of 10s 0d per hogshead was enacted in 1753 and the apple trees soon supplied no more than local needs.

Yet the War of American Independence was at its height, the county's ports were crowded with ships and soldiers and doubtless there was a demand for farm produce.

Of the population of between 350 and 400, about 150 lived in Thurlestone and 100 in Buckland. Bantham had little more than a row of fishermen's cottages and some boathouses. The tax returns indicate six principal owners who between them paid more than half the total sum and forty-eight others who contributed the remainder, some as little as a few shillings for a cottage. Many of their homes, or at least the walls and thatched roofs, have survived and may be seen in the village street at Thurlestone and in the hamlet of Buckland. Bantham Ham, upon which '. . . 5 of my Lords Tenants heretofore particularly mentioned have the right to turn 70 sheep and Mr. Longman the right to turn two sheep . . . ' (presumably 352 in all) in 1777 is now a popular bathing area and Bantham itself is a thriving hamlet.

The parish registers give a fair indication of the social structure. Nine men had the prefix 'Mr' and three of their wives were designated 'Mrs'. Mr. Thomas Square and Mr. William Adams had their homes opposite the church, on land extending up to the present Thurlestone Hotel, and grazed their sheep along the coastal strip which is now the golf course. Mr James Polybank farmed his acres around Whitley, his house still standing beside the road on the way to Kingsbridge. William Adam's brother John lived in Clannacombe, much the most impressive residence in the parish. Originally an ecclesiastical house of rest, this large Elizabethan mansion belonged to the Phillips family from 1651, later passing to the Adams and then, in the early 1800s, to the descendants of Thomas Square. It never belonged to the Courtenay Estates.

Mr William Cornish, whose family name, along with the Bevells, occurs frequently in the earliest registers of 1558-70, managed an estate in the fertile Aune valley above Bantham. Nobody above the rank of 'Mr' was entered in the registers at any time. Occasionally, 'Gentlemen' were recorded as such, probably in recognition of their educational distinction, the sole example in 1777 being James Wakeham, whose gentility was recognised at his marriage and at the baptisms of his children and who had been promoted 'Mr' by the time of his burial in 1795. These various parishioners all came from families whose surnames were already well established in the years 1650-99. Less exalted were the minor gentry, yeomen, tenant farmers, husbandmen and artisans. Yeomen and husbandmen comprised about two-thirds of the men according to the occupations listed in the burial register. The Courtenay survey describes twenty residences as 'house, outhouses, court and garden', usually with a small apple orchard beyond the garden. Two of them, John Shepherd's tenement and Hingston's cottage remain substantially unchanged just above the lower village shop in Thurlestone. Many of the cottages have survived from 1777, when they housed some of the Lidstones, Hardys, Wakehams, Phillips, Wordens and Shepherds listed in the table. Perhaps the most interesting are the cottages above the Old Rectory.They were originally built as the church house for the holding of meetings and festivities, but were converted into dwellings when the Puritans of the seventeenth century objected to revelry in such places. Reminders of former activities include Hugh Date's Thurlestone mill and forge, beside the stream at Buckland, now a butcher's shop, and a large apple press at Clannacombe.

The absence of heath and moorland meant that virtually the whole of the parish was available for cultivation and the raising of sheep, cattle and domestic animals. Maybe some farms were managed more efficiently than others, but at least many of the villagers had homes they could call their own and few families were isolated from the social intercourse of the parochial community.

FAMILY RECONSTITUTION

Prominent Families			*Notable Lineages*		
	Baptisms by name	Total baptisms	Marriages	Descendants	Years
Lidstone	142	217	John and Elizabeth Lidstone	68	1650-1868
Moore	156	240	John Moore and Abigail Randall	171	1691-1939
Hardy	123	179	Hugh and Prothesa Hardy	150	1671-1868
Phillips	72	151			
Randall	23	252	Roger and Alice Randall	205	1657-1935
Shepherd	79	239			
Tabb	43	154	John and Sarah Tabb	151	1700-1935
Worden	66	220			
Higston	63	161	Joseph Hingston and Elizabeth Worden	159	1710-1936
Clark	45	158	Walter Clark and Elizabeth Hingston	80	1776-1935
Hannaford	46	155	James Hannaford Mary Sheriff	88	1799-1945

Index